"LATE NIGHT WITH DAVID LETTERMAN"

BOOK OF
TOP TEN
LISTS

David Letterman and the
"Late Night with David Letterman" Writers

POCKET BOOKS

New York   London   Toronto   Sydney   Tokyo   Singapore

An excerpt from the book appeared in *Playboy* Magazine.

POCKET BOOKS, a division of Simon & Schuster Inc.
1230 Avenue of the Americas, New York, NY 10020

ISBN: 0-671-51143-2

First Pocket Books paperback printing November 1994

10 9 8 7 6 5 4 3 2

POCKET and colophon are registered trademarks of
Simon & Schuster Inc.

Printed in the U.S.A.

ACKNOWLEDGMENTS

Thanks to:

Leslie Wells

Maria Pope

Joe Furey

Pami Shamir

Ellen Cowhey.

Special thanks to the faculty, alumni, and student body of the United States Merchant Marine Academy.

FOREWORD

"Yes I do!" is the reply that will leap smartly from your heart and proudly from your lips the next time someone asks, "Do you believe in miracles?" And take it from me—you will after you read this compelling, insightful stand-up-and-salute account of the 1980 United States Olympic Hockey Team's (mere boys, actually) fairy-tale victory over the fearsome Soviet Olympic juggernaut. A team so powerful, hockey experts then and now routinely did and do describe it as a juggernaut. If you love Olympic hockey, then this is the book for you. What about the rumor that the Americans were forced to play on old or borrowed skates? Well, it turns out not to be true. But consider this: What if it was? How did the world of sports react to this stunning and unparalleled upset? Typical of the response is this quote from one-time New York Mets second base-man Felix Milan, who enjoyed the contest from his home near Fort Meyers, Florida: "I really didn't think they had a chance."

If you weren't one of the lucky thousands to witness this miracle live at rinkside in Lake Placid, or one of the many millions who enjoyed tape-delayed coverage in its entirety, or video highlights on one of the fine network or local news programs, then this is the book you'll want to purchase again and again just so you'll be able to look yourself in the mirror and say, "I own several copies, Jim." The National Council of Churches urges that this book be read aloud to the family at appropriate, meaningful times of the year—but should in no way take the place of—or interfere with—traditional forms of worship. Please read this wonderful little book. You'll thank me later.

Dave Letterman

INTRODUCTION

By the time you read this, I will already be dead.

No, no! I'm fine. Everything's okay. I just wanted to make sure you were paying attention to these little prefaces or forewords or whatever the hell they are. Lord knows, it would be all too easy for you to just plunge right in and start reading the Top Ten Lists themselves and just skip the introduction—betraying yourself for what you are, which is little better than an animal.

Now, a word about how what you're holding in your hand got to be there. (I pray to God all you're holding is this book.) Recently, Dave Letterman and I went into our local bookstore and took a look around—a *good* look around. Let me tell you, we were shocked and dismayed by what we saw. *There just weren't enough books for sale.* That's when we decided to do something. We decided to eat a hearty lunch and nap in our offices until quitting time. About a week later, it occurred to me: Why, *we could put out a book of our own!*

But what about all the hard work and long hours such a project would entail? Well, I remembered that the so-called "experts" had said the same thing about doing a TV show—and that turned out to be a lot of nonsense. We could probably produce something as quickly and with as little effort as our nightly telecast.

My suggestion was greeted with enthusiasm at the weekly board meeting in Dave's garage. It even inspired some wild speculations about extending the plan to include a line of Letterman adhesive bandages and a summer camp for overweight teens.

By midafternoon, this book was rolling off the presses. We couldn't be more proud.

Sorry about scaring you before!

Steve O'Donnell
Head Writer,
"Late Night With David Letterman"

TOP TEN WORDS THAT ALMOST RHYME WITH "PEAS"

10. Heats

9. Rice

8. Moss

7. Ties

6. Needs

5. Lens

4. Ice

3. Nurse

2. Leaks

1. Meats

TOP TEN THINGS
OVERHEARD ON
OUR FIRST SHOW

10. "I think he used to play Chip on 'My Three Sons' "

9. "It would be a shame if that band leader ever lost his magnificent head of hair"

8. "My name is Dave—and I'm here to sing! Sing! Sing!"

7. "Oh no! Not Kamarr the Magician"

6. "You can't come in here, Mr. Snyder. Your show was cancelled"

5. "When's he gonna take out those gag teeth?"

4. "Can you use the restroom upstairs? We're doing a show in here"

3. "I can't believe Lord Melman would stoop to doing American television"

2. "I sat through the show. Now where's my tote bag?"

1. "He's no Dinah"

TOP TEN AMISH PICKUP LINES

10. Are thee at barn-raisings often?

9. If our religion didn't forbid the use of telephones, I would ask thee for thy number

8. Can I buy thee a buttermilk colada?

7. You've really got the build for that plain bonnet and shapeless black dress

6. Say, my favorite movie is *Witness* too!

5. Are thee a model?

4. There are so many phonies at these quilting bees. Let's go someplace quiet

3. Thy buggy has a bitchin' lacquer job

2. I got Sinatra tickets

1. Are thee up for some plowing?

BATMAN'S TOP TEN PET PEEVES

10. After dramatic entrance at scene of crime, having to convince everybody he's not a professional wrestler

9. When you can see the outline of his underwear through the Bat suit

8. Punks who gather around and smart off while he's getting gas for the Batmobile

7. Nuclear power source for utility belt has rendered him sterile

6. When really stupid people shout out, "Hey! Where's Tonto?"

5. When dry cleaner accidentally switches Bat suit and San Diego Chicken costume

4. When an episode focuses way too much on Jake (Oh, I'm sorry. That's one of the pet peeves of the "Fatman")

3. Seeing Alfred the butler talking to Albert Goldman

2. The way any two-bit moron with a flashlight and a piece of cardboard can summon him at night

1. When people call him *The* Batman." It's just "Batman," damn it!

TOP TEN LEAST POPULAR
BEN & JERRY'S
ICE CREAM FLAVORS

10. Oprah Mocha

9. Raspberry Rash

8. Norieggnog

7. Cholesterol Chip

6. Zsa Zsa Gaboreo

5. Tiny Filaments o' Tungsten

4. Vap-O-Rub

3. Stuff-Found-in-Ben-&-Jerry's-Pockets

2. Bus Depot Fudge

1. Hitler Ripple

TOP TEN COMMERCIAL
CASKET MODELS

10. The Dirt-Master

 9. Tupper-Tomb

 8. Krazy-Kasket from Whammo

 7. The Slim Reaper

 6. The 19th Hole

 5. McCoffin Styrofoam Casket

 4. The Comfort-King Velvetliner (endorsed by Paul Anka)

 3. Cap'n Crypt

 2. The Cardboard Warrior

 1. The La-Z-Boy Eterna-Lounger

TOP TEN NEW ADVERTISING SLOGANS FOR DELTA AIRLINES

10. We're Amtrak with Wings

9. Join Our Frequent Near-Miss Program

8. Ask About Our Out-of-Court Settlements

7. Noisy Engines? We'll Turn 'Em Off!

6. Complimentary Champagne in Free-Fall

5. Enjoy the In-Flight Movie on the Plane Next to You

4. The Kids Will Love Our Inflatable Slides

3. Terrorists Are Afraid to Fly with Us

2. Our Pilots Are Terminally Ill and Have Nothing to Lose

1. We Might Be Landing on Your Street!

TOP TEN LEAST POPULAR
FAIRY TALES

10. The Gingerbread Man Chews Off His Own Leg to Get Out of a Bear Trap

9. Geraldo and Gretel

8. The Ugly Duckling Who Had Liposuction and Cheek Implants

7. The Little Old Lady Who Lived in Al Sharpton's Hair

6. The Big Dragon with Intestinal Distress

5. Mike Tyson Whips the Hell Out of the Little People

4. Scrappy, the Very Contagious Monkey

3. George Bush Won't Raise Taxes

2. The Little Engine that Occasionally Couldn't

1. Goldilocks and the Tainted Clams

TOP TEN CAMPAIGN PROMISES GEORGE BUSH IS SORRY HE MADE

10. To use Star Wars satellites to give everybody free HBO

9. To bite head off rat at first press conference

8. To bomb France back to the Stone Age

7. To get to the bottom of this whole Bigfoot thing

6. To appease tobacco lobby by always having picture taken with cigarette in mouth

5. To deflower Brooke Shields on board the space shuttle *Atlantis*

4. To dispose of radioactive waste through the Home Shopping Network

3. At summit with Soviets, to try "pull my finger" trick on Gorbachev

2. To bring more lightweight pretty-boys into the executive branch

1. To reveal during inaugural address the whereabouts of Elvis

TOP TEN CANINE DISORDERS OR DEBUTANTE COMPLAINTS

10. Distemper

9. Rabies

8. Broken heel

7. Wilted corsage

6. Mange

5. Out of shrimp

4. Heartworms

3. Warm Tab

2. Ticks

1. Kennel cough/Daddy's drunk   *(tie)*

TOP TEN CHAPTER TITLES FROM SHIRLEY MacLAINE'S NEW BOOK

10. My Years with the White Sox

9. Pizza to Go—from Alpha Centauri

8. Leif Erikson: Lousy in the Sack

7. I Go Completely Nuts and Start Writing Books

6. I Was the 1,378,000th Burger Sold at McDonald's

5. Flying Saucers: More Dependable than Eastern

4. The Voices in My Head Argue Over Their Share of the Book Royalties

3. Is that a Crystal in Your Pocket or Are You Just Glad to See Me?

2. Didn't I Already Write This Chapter?

1. *I'm* Crazy? You Spent $21.95 on This Book!

TOP TEN CHRISTMAS MOVIES IN TIMES SQUARE

10. *Hot Buttered Elves*

9. *Santa's Magic Lap*

8. *Babes in Boyland*

7. *Crisco Kringle*

6. *Yes, Yes, Oh God Yes, Virginia*

5. *Ninja Reindeer Killfest '88*

4. *Not-So-Tiny Tim*

3. *Santa Goes 'Round-the-World*

2. *The Nutcracker Swede*

1. *I'm Not Rudolph; That's Not My Nose*

TOP TEN COMPLAINTS BY COMIC STRIP CHARACTERS

10. Buried in back of the newspaper

9. Have to share page with horoscope

8. Word balloon causes pressure on head

7. Body out of proportion

6. Poor sex life

5. Asked out on date by Sluggo

4. Dizziness, vomiting from smell of newsprint

3. Mary Worth is "a real bringdown"

2. Garfield smells bad

1. I don't have thumbs

TOP TEN COOL THINGS
ABOUT THE DRUIDS

10. They used Stonehenge for their ceremonies

9. They regarded oak and mistletoe as sacred

8. They wore scary-looking hooded robes

7. They said "please" and "thank you" before and after human sacrifice

6. They studied the flights of birds to predict the future without the aid of a daily syndicated horoscope column

5. They kept hot drinks hot, cool drinks cool

4. They made fun of Roman soldiers wearing skirts

3. They sometimes worshipped a giant statue of Ray Charles

2. They claimed to be "born to lose"

1. They died out in the early fifth century/ they partied like it was 1999   *(tie)*

TOP TEN NICKNAMES FOR JACK KLUGMAN

10. Jackie

9. Klug

8. Klugger

7. The Klugmeister

6. Oscar/Quincy

5. Buzz

4. Cowboy

3. Spud

2. Dink

1. Cap'n

TOP TEN COURSES FOR ATHLETES AT SMU

10. Subtraction: Addition's Tricky Pal

9. The First 30 Pages of *A Tale of Two Cities:* Foundation of a Classic

8. Sandwich-making (final project required)

7. Alumni-owned Hotels, Restaurants and Car Dealerships: The Interlocking Economy

6. Pre-Law Seminar: Age of Consent in the 50 States

5. The Denny's Menu: Recent Discoveries

4. The Bunny and the Wolf: Hand Shadow Workshop

3. Draw Winky

2. From *First Love* to *Looker:* The Films in Which Susan Dey Appears Naked

1. The Poetry of Hank Stram

DAN QUAYLE'S TOP TEN NATIONAL GUARD DUTIES

10. Make sure Armory's vending machines never run out of pretzel sticks

9. Look through catalogs for cute gifts for officers' wives

8. Enforce "no horseplay" rule at public pools

7. Play hula girl on skit night

6. Make sure hot side stays hot, cool side cool

5. Make cool explosion sounds when platoon trains with dummy grenades

4. Beat local Scout troops to best lakeside campsites

3. Keep guys without shirts from entering 7-Elevens

2. Write to Nancy Sinatra; urge her to visit base

1. Round-the-clock blob watch

LIBYA'S TOP TEN DEROGATORY TERMS FOR AMERICANS

10. Imperialist Pigs

9. Yankee Jackals

8. Milkshake-Swilling Devils

7. Bowling-Addicted Hyenas

6. Fess Parkers

5. Steak-Gorged Gunslingers

4. Red-White-and-Goofies

3. Hedge-Trimming Elvis-Lovers

2. Beardless Buick Jockeys

1. Golfshoe Geeks

TOP TEN DISADVANTAGES OF WINNING A NOBEL PRIZE

10. Have to get kissed by herring-breathed King Olaf

9. Automatically disqualifies you from being contestant on "Jeopardy"

8. Dangling medallion could get caught in open blender

7. More junk mail from fly-by-night award-polishing services

6. Distant relatives pestering you for free advice on particle physics

5. Have to get in embarrassing kickline at end of ceremony with other winners

4. Friends always borrowing medal for 10% discount at participating Red Lobsters

3. Run-ins with gangs of Pulitzer Prize winners usually end up in a brawl

2. Sarcasm of postman when he says, "Here's your new copy of *Big Jugs* magazine, Mr. Nobel Laureate."

1. Don't see a dime from Mattel Nobel Prize action figures

TOP TEN DUKAKIS EXCUSES

10. Forgot to wear "lucky" shorts

9. Thought election was first Tuesday in *December*

8. It's just a big popularity contest

7. Used Wendell to warm up campaign crowds

6. Couldn't believe anyone in a million, jillion years would vote for George Bush

5. Extensive campaigning in Belgium was waste of time

4. Fell for Bush's old "You-vote-for-me-and-I'll-vote-for-you" trick

3. *Insert your own eyebrow joke here*

2. Ill-advised pledge to "tax you bastards back to the Stone Age"

1. Didn't care about Presidency; just wanted to win $20 bet that I could do better than Mondale

TOP TEN DUTIES OF MY ASSISTANT LAURIE DIAMOND

10. Call Mom on major holidays and play tape of me wishing her the best

9. Reserve steam room for my weekly current events discussion with Mike Tyson

8. Apologize to guests from night before

7. Keep me updated on what's happening in "Marmaduke" comic strip

6. Research retail price of gifts given to me by staffers

5. Scan lost & found columns for any sign of the monkey-fur jumpsuit

4. Steam uncanceled stamps off fan mail

3. Some minor surgery

2. Monitor Italian sex magazines for any mention of me

1. Help me get my money back from those liars over at Tastee-Freeze

TOP TEN LEAST POPULAR EXHIBITS AT THE BASEBALL HALL OF FAME

10. The Tobacco Juice Fountain and Reflecting Pool

9. Babe Ruth's cup

8. What-It's-Like-to-Get-Hit-in-the-Head-with-a-Nolan-Ryan-Fastball

7. The Yogi Berra Kissing Booth

6. The giant stack of Pete Rose's losing OTB tickets

5. Display case of garbage thrown at the San Diego Chicken

4. Steve Garvey's bed and on-deck circle

3. Cocktail glass filled with Billy Martin's knocked-out teeth

2. Scratch-a-Real-Big-Leaguer

1. The Audioanimatronic Mookie

BERNHARD GOETZ'S TOP TEN PICKUP LINES

10. Excuse me, miss. I was shooting at the gentleman next to you

9. How'd you like to double date with the Sliwas?

8. Care to dance with an intense, gun-toting loner?

7. You would have a very curvy chalk outline

6. I hate these pistol ranges. They're just meat markets

5. Sure—I know Gabe Pressman *personally*

4. Give me a scotch and soda and see what the punk on the floor will have

3. Which do you think is funnier—*Deathwish 2* or *Deathwish 3?*

2. The evening is young. Let's clean up this town

1. That *is* a gun in my pocket and I *am* glad to see you

TOP TEN THINGS OVERHEARD AT THE MOSCOW McDONALD'S

10. "You want turnips with that?"

9. "I'm spending three weeks' salary for this Happy Meal."

8. "The food was better in the gulag."

7. "In nine or ten years, when you do get a car, you'll really appreciate the drive-thru window."

6. "Excuse me, comrade—my cold side is cold . . . but so is my hot side!"

5. "This sure beats driving a New York City cab."

4. "Volkov, KGB—What's in the secret sauce?"

3. "I'm sorry, Mrs. Gorbachev, we're not hiring."

2. "There go our Olympic hopes."

1. "This sucks. Let's go to White Castle."

TOP TEN ELF COMPLAINTS

10. Bells on clothing target for jeers at truck stops

9. Need two pieces of I.D. to buy beer

8. Santa's union-busting goons killed a guy last spring

7. Black elves control weight room

6. R&R weekends in Aleutians spoiled by trigger-happy shore patrol

5. Incredible markup at North Pole 7-Eleven

4. Workmen's compensation doesn't cover "mistletoe lung"

3. The Colonel practically runs my life (Sorry, that's an Elvis complaint)

2. Dead elves just tossed out on tundra

1. Santa only invites his favorites to join him in the Jacuzzi

TOP TEN EXCUSES OF THE EXXON TANKER CAPTAIN

10. Was trying to scrape ice off reef for margarita

9. Thought harbor was filled with the soft, fluffy kind of rocks

8. Felt flourishing salmon population was getting a little cocky lately

7. Wanted to impress Jodie Foster

6. Kept drinking beer to wash away taste of cheap scotch

5. First mate and I were having "tastes great/less filling" argument

4. Swerving to avoid oncoming Eastern Airlines jet

3. You really need a good nap after downing a pitcher of frozen daiquiris

2. Hoping to dislodge any whales that might be trapped in ice

1. Man, was I *'faced!*

BIGFOOT'S TOP TEN
PET PEEVES

10. Fat guys who lounge around the campground shirtless

9. Nobody ever goes after Alf with tranquilizer darts

8. Chicks who have a hang-up about lice-infested body hair

7. This Dan Quayle jerk

6. Kids today would rather see the San Diego Chicken

5. Lead role in *The Ed Asner Story* never materialized

4. The way squirrels smell when they're damp

3. Elvis always drops by right before dinner

2. Honking Winnebagos while you're trying to enjoy road kill

1. Driver's license photo makes him look like Gregg Allman

TOP TEN LEAST-KNOWN NORMAN ROCKWELL PAINTINGS

10. A Boy's First Manicure

9. The Old Hobo's Infected Foot

8. The Circus Geek and the Cub Scout

7. Caught Touching Himself

6. Sniper in the Mall

5. Sweetheart of the Cell-Block

4. Christmas at the Hair Club for Men

3. Andrew Wyeth Nails Helga

2. Bad Clams

1. Turn Your Head and Cough

TOP TEN EXPRESSIONS
THAT SOUND DIRTY
BUT REALLY AREN'T

10. Frosting the Pastry

 9. Shooting Hoops

 8. Jumping the Turnstile

 7. Checking Your Oil

 6. Tethering the Blimp

 5. Sending Out for Sushi

 4. Picnic on the Grass

 3. Quarter-Pounder at the Golden Arches

 2. Shaking Hands with Abraham Lincoln

 1. Wind-Surfing on Mount Baldy

FAWN HALL'S TOP TEN TURN-ONS

10. Guys with cute code names

9. Rebel leaders who send a card for no special reason

8. *Anything* in camouflage

7. Heavy petting under sodium pentathol

6. Guys with their own private armies

5. Death squad members who aren't afraid to cry sometimes

4. Guys who leave their medals on

3. People in really goofy costumes who jump up and down (Oh, sorry, that's a *Monty* Hall turn-on)

2. Sitting on the paper shredder when it's going full speed

1. Sharing a quiet moment with a known national security risk

TOP TEN FEARS OF McDONALD'S MANAGERS

10. Under excruciating torture, I might reveal ingredients of secret sauce

9. Customers will figure out fish sandwich and apple pie are exact same item

8. Mayor McCheese's nude, lifeless body will be found in a cheap hotel room somewhere down south

7. Might someday accidentally eat a McNugget

6. After sex with wife, might mistakenly say, "Do you want fries with that?"

5. One of the trainees wants to man the shake machine and damn it—he's not ready!

4. Something will happen to Bush

3. Even after selling a billion Big Macs, I'll still feel kind of empty inside

2. Someday a race of supercows will make paper-thin burgers out of *me*

1. That might not be mayonnaise

TOP TEN CARNIVAL PICKUP LINES

10. I couldn't help noticing you throw up on the Tilt-a-Whirl

9. Is somebody frying dough or is that you?

8. But I have to put my hands there to guess your weight

7. I get off at nine, Senator Tower

6. After a nice candlelit dinner, I'll let you pound a nail into my head

5. I'm sure I've got a tattoo of your name on me somewhere

4. How'd you like to become *Mrs.* Torso?

3. *Insert your own corndog joke here*

2. You know, if you didn't have that hard squinty look so common to carnival trash, you could be a model

1. Is that a ring toss game—or are you just glad to see me?

TOP TEN FEATURES OF THE NEW STEALTH BOMBER

10. Has two-inch ball hitch on back so it can pull Stealth trailer

9. Makes square and crescent-shaped ice cubes

8. Plenty of room on wing for Trump logo

7. Computer tabulator shows pilot up-to-the-minute frequent flyer mileage

6. Easiest plane ever for pouring Pepsi upside down

5. Siren sounds if monster appears on wing, like in "Twilight Zone"

4. Nose cone opens to release giant spring-loaded boxing glove

3. Enormous speakers can be heard playing "We Will Rock You" across a continent

2. Advanced bombsights allow crew to deliver payload right down Khaddafy's shorts

1. Kids fly free

TOP TEN GENERAL ELECTRIC PRODUCTS IN DEVELOPMENT

10. Artificial appendix

9. Electric dreadlock de-tangler

8. TV audio system that automatically adds an Italian accent

7. 3-speed back shaver

6. Secret beam that causes brains of Sylvania executives to balloon up until they burst

5. Telephone voice modulator that makes you sound like Alex Trebek

4. TV screen that makes every Cosby kid look black

3. New patio for Robert C. Wright's house

2. Zombie monkeys who operate waffle iron

1. The vibrating pocket-buddy

TOP TEN GOOD THINGS ABOUT THE GREENHOUSE EFFECT

10. Melting polar ice caps make for better surfing

9. Long lines at Disney World reduced by sunstroke

8. Within five years, Jerry Lewis's hair will be bone-dry

7. Can use "stuck in road tar" as acceptable excuse for missing work

6. ABC will take a 200-million-dollar bath on Winter Olympics

5. Intense heat should open pores in General Noriega's forehead

4. My dog-shaving business will take off

3. "I'm dehydrated" will replace "I'm not gonna pay a lot for this muffler" as America's favorite phrase

2. Can cook lobster by lowering it into toilet

1. Hot babes, less clothes. 'Nuff said

TOP TEN HEADLINES
IN HELL

10. Hitler Welcomes Mengele in Touching Ceremony

9. Icewater Canceled—Again!

8. Slumbering Carnivorous Worms Awaken in Very Bad Mood

7. Authorities Announce: Everything to Feel "Itchier"

6. Satan Vows: Steinbrenner's My Man for the Entire Season

5. Roy Cohn to Host Networking Barbecue

4. Most Residents Prefer Flame-Broiling to Frying

3. Muzak to Feature "Up with People" for Rest of Eternity

2. Welcoming Party for Ayatollah Best Ever

1. We're Getting Cable!

TOP TEN FEARS OF SNUGGLES THE FABRIC SOFTENER BEAR

10. Might someday have to chew own leg off to escape from lint trap

9. Sleeping in laundry basket exposes him to attack by housecats

8. He may wind up in a washer with Al Sharpton's undershirts

7. People will find out about that mauled camper back in '78

6. Excess softener will leave him unable to perform as a male

5. First wife Joey Heatherton will write book claiming he beat her regularly

4. Winnie-the-Pooh will get drunk at family gathering and start loudly suggesting that *he* should be the Fabric Softener Bear

3. Something might happen to George Bush

2. Company doctors will perform some kind of surgery to insure he remains "snuggly" forever

1. The Pillsbury Doughboy will ask him to poke lower

TOP TEN HEADLINES THAT WOULD START A PANIC

10. Casey Kasem Builds Own Nuclear Device

9. Yanks Swap Mattingly for Eve Arden

8. Walking Dead Stalk City, Demand Soul Kisses

7. It Turns Out You Really Need Your Tonsils

6. Seals & Croft, Brewer & Shipley to Form Supergroup

5. Nell Carter, *Playboy* Magazine Reach Terms

4. Constitution Thrown Out in Favor of Old "Marmaduke" Cartoon

3. "Sometimes When We Touch" Made National Anthem

2. Willie Nelson Discovered Washing Hair in New York City Water Supply

1. "Late Night" to Begin Top Twenty Lists

ELVIS PRESLEY'S TOP TEN
HOUSEHOLD HINTS

10. A little club soda will get food stains out of satin capes

9. Bargain metal polishes may discolor your solid gold piano

8. Use blow-dryer to speed up defrosting time on TV dinners

7. A wad of gum will keep your medallion from sliding around your chest

6. Stubborn stain on auto upholstery? Buy a new car

5. Jewel-encrusted belts make good emergency snow treads

4. Put Las Vegas souvenirs on mantel for that "museum" effect

3. Out of hair spray? Try PAM

2. For a classy dessert, remove sticks from Eskimo Pies before serving

1. A small handgun makes any TV remote control

TOP TEN ELF PICKUP LINES

10. I'm down here

9. Just because I've got bells on my shoes doesn't mean I'm a sissy

8. I was once a lawn ornament for Jon Bon Jovi

7. I can get you off the naughty list

6. I have certain needs that can't be satisfied by working on toys

5. I'm a magical being. Take off your bra

4. No, no. I don't bake cookies. You're thinking of those dorks over at Keebler

3. I get a thimbleful of tequila in me and I turn into a wild man

2. You'd look great in a Raggedy Ann wig

1. I can eat my weight in cocktail wieners

TEN TOP IRANIAN T-SHIRT SLOGANS

10. Iraq Busters

9. Surf Straits of Hormuz

8. Mom and Dad Blew Up a Busload of Tourists, and All I Got Was This Lousy T-shirt

7. Death to All Americans—Except Mötley Crüe

6. Official Veil Inspector

5. Kiss Me, I'm a Walking Time Bomb

4. I've Been Tested for Sand Chiggers

3. You Don't Have to Be Crazy to Set Yourself on Fire & Run into an Enemy Tank—But It Sure Helps!

2. If You Don't Ride a Camel, You Ain't Shiite

1. Spuds Khomeini: The Original Party Animal

TOP TEN CHRISTMAS TIPS FROM GENERAL ELECTRIC

10. If one light bulb in your house goes out, replace them all

9. Fluorescent tubes make great Star Wars swords for the kids

8. Blow-dryers can be used to keep food warm

7. Big corporations shouldn't commercialize this blessed season by handing out bonuses

6. Keeping several TVs and radios on all the time creates a feeling of warmth and intimacy

5. We heard that Sylvania bulbs give off some kind of poison gas

4. Same deal with Westinghouse

3. Electric toothbrushes should be left on all day to keep them loose

2. A G.E. industrial turbine makes a one-of-a-kind stocking stuffer

1. Warranties, like greeting cards, should be thrown out

TOP TEN INDY 500 PIT CREW PET PEEVES

10. Drivers who want a free NFL mug with every fill-up

9. Being played in the movies by Jim Nabors

8. Racers in such a hurry to get out of pit they run over your origami birds

7. For the rest of your life, any time you're in a car that gets a flat, everyone just assumes that you should fix it

6. They keep blacking out the good parts of the Rob Lowe video

5. It's hard to pick up chicks while reeking of methane

4. The way those suction-cup Garfield dolls fall off at 230 miles per hour

3. Joke T-shirts that say "Pit Crew Guys Do It in Seven Seconds"

2. Really big dogs who get themselves booked on TV shows and then don't show up

1. Those pansies at Jiffy-Lube

JAMES BROWN'S TOP TEN PRISON COMPLAINTS

10. Only two hair dryers for over 3,000 men!

9. Guards keep calling me "Little Richard"

8. Always getting leg caught in bars when doing the splits

7. Five packs of cigarettes for one bottle of Luster-Silk!

6. Prison library scandalously short of Jane Austen novels

5. Escape tunnel too narrow to shimmy in

4. Irritating snoring of Ike Turner

3. Death row guys always win talent show because of sympathy vote

2. Can't believe I'm in here and John Denver walks around free

1. Just hate being soul brother #175683

JIM BAKKER'S TOP TEN PICKUP LINES

10. Pray here often?

9. Your eyes are the same color as my leisure suit

8. Let me give you my 800 number

7. What's your favorite—Old or New Testament?

6. I can give you a lift as far as Charlotte

5. If I don't get two million women by June first, God will kill me

4. But you're not married to your cousin *yet*

3. I look like a frog, but I love like a stallion

2. You're not Jewish, are you?

1. Tiffany Lurlene? Why, that was my mother's name!

TOP TEN JOB TITLES ON KURT WALDHEIM'S RESUME

10. Secretary-General, United Nations (1972)

9. Austrian Presidential candidate (1986)

8. Officer, Diplomatic Corps (1946)

7. German Army translator (1939)

6. Second Clarinet, Panzer Auxiliary Band (1943)

5. Volunteer coach, Little Aryans softball league (1935)

4. Treasurer, Luftwaffe Pep Club (1944)

3. Fashion consultant, Brown Shirts (1932)

2. *(I can't quite make out number 2—apparently it's been erased)*

1. Dessert chef, "The Bunker" (1945)

CLEVELAND INDIAN PLAYERS' TOP TEN EXCUSES

10. Lost it in the lights

9. Thought ball would go foul

8. Ball took a wicked hop

7. Thought *you* had it

6. Fumes from artificial turf made me woozy

5. Feelings hurt by jeers of so-called fans

4. Had one of my spells

3. Just couldn't get Michelob Light jingle out of my head

2. Had bad clams for lunch

1. Distracted by high-pitched sounds only I can hear

SUBWAY PUNKS' TOP TEN ETIQUETTE TIPS

10. When passing a sharpened screwdriver to a friend, remember—it's *handle first*

9. Don't be selfish; share your radio music with everyone in the car

8. Always say, "Could I have five dollars, *please?*"

7. Allow your elders and ladies to jump turnstile ahead of you

6. Lookouts work as hard as anybody; a 15% gratuity is customary

5. Don't embarrass a victim by pointing out a fake Rolex

4. When two wolf packs meet in a car, the group moving from front to rear has the right of way

3. Victims who don't press charges deserve a nice thank-you note

2. Learning a few phrases in a foreign language can save you minutes of fruitless shoving and slapping

1. Don't be greedy; leave some valuables for the next gang of toughs

TOP TEN COMPLAINTS OF NEW YORK CITY COPS

10. Police-band radio: too much talk, not enough rock

9. Shoulder holster can only hold three doughnuts

8. Out-of-towners undertip

7. Jackie Onassis always kicks out windows in back of cruiser

6. Winter uniforms "too dowdy"

5. Not allowed to sell Amway products on beat

4. Forced to look the other way when Mayor "greets Merv Griffin"

3. Later novels of Thackeray failed to live up to promise of his early works

2. Only nice girls we meet are criminals

1. Commissioner too quick to call in Batman

DAVE LETTERMAN'S TOP TEN DRIVING TIPS

10. Firemen like it when you race alongside them

9. If pursued by highway patrol, always pull over immediately, then try to flee on foot

8. Keep freezer bags in glove compartment in case you hit a steer

7. With the right tools, any rental car can be a convertible

6. When transporting a monkey, don't let him take the wheel no matter how much he screeches

5. To let other drivers know you are there, start blowing your horn as you leave the driveway & don't stop until you reach your destination

4. Only use Bat chutes in a real emergency

3. An engineer's cap and bandana add an element of fantasy and fun

2. There are no finer men and women than the officers of the New Canaan, Connecticut, police dept. They are the unsung heroes of the twentieth century

1. When cutting through yards at night, look out for kids in tents

TOP TEN "DEAR ABBY" LETTER SIGNATURES

10. Bewildered in Baltimore

9. Can't Sit Down in San Pedro

8. Female, Bearded and Happy

7. Bitter Soon-to-Be-Divorced Former Swedish Rock Star

6. Mr. Pelican Pants

5. Naked in James Garner's Garage

4. A Cleveland Baseball Team

3. Bryant Gumbel

2. In Prison and Loving It

1. P-Whipped in the White House

JOHN GOTTI'S TOP TEN TAX TIPS

10. You can deduct the entire piano even if you bought it just for the wire

9. Guys who escape from the trunk of your car may be considered business losses

8. No matter how much he relies on your business, a funeral director does not count as a dependent

7. Another write-off: long-distance calls to Pete Rose

6. You must actually kill someone in your home for it to qualify as "place of business"

5. Three simple words to the auditor: "How's your family?"

4. For a vacation to count as a business trip, return with 100 pounds of heroin

3. Smart-guy talk show hosts may end up with more medical expenses than they thought

2. When reporting income, be plausible. No pizzeria in the world takes in 3 billion dollars a day

1. What H&R Block can't do, cement blocks can

TOP TEN CHILDREN'S BOOKS NOT RECOMMENDED BY THE NATIONAL LIBRARY ASSOCIATION

10. *Curious George and the High-Voltage Fence*

9. *The Boy Who Died from Eating All His Vegetables*

8. *Legends of Scab Football*

7. *Teddy: The Elf with a Detached Retina*

6. *Tommy Tune: Boy Choreographer*

5. *Joe Garagiola Retells Favorite Fairy Tales but Can't Remember the Endings to All of Them*

4. *Ed Beckley's Start a Real Estate Empire with Change from Mom's Purse*

3. *Things Rich Kids Have That You Never Will*

2. *Let's Draw Betty and Veronica with Their Clothes Off*

1. *The Care Bears Maul Some Campers and Are Shot Dead*

TOP TEN SOURCES OF FRICTION IN THE ARNOLD SCHWARZENEGGER–MARIA SHRIVER MARRIAGE

10. Language barrier

9. Forrest Sawyer drops in at all hours

8. Puts steroids in mint dish as practical joke

7. Uncle Ted always wants to arm wrestle

6. Thinks Jane Pauley is a "fabulous babe"

5. Refuses to learn words to "Edelweiss"

4. Muscle magazines leave no room in rack for *Town & Country*

3. Uses "bulking up" as excuse to eat like a pig

2. Rose always wants to arm wrestle

1. Body oil on the upholstery

TOP TEN LEAST POPULAR CANDY BARS

10. Lug Nut

9. Turkish Prison Taffy

8. Hardened Toothpaste Mint Patties

7. Sunoco Resin Chews

6. Reverend Al's Marshmallow Medallions

5. Mexican Monkey Brittle

4. Good 'N' Linty

3. Two Musketeers and a Guy with a Hacking Cough

2. Mookie Way

1. Roger Ebert's Mystery Log

DAN QUAYLE'S TOP TEN PICKUP LINES

10. Didn't we almost flunk out of school together?

9. How about a drink with a historical footnote?

8. I sure would have gone to Vietnam if the Cong looked like you

7. Can my father buy you a drink?

6. You could close your eyes and pretend I'm Jack Kemp

5. I think I saw Elvis last week at the Stuckey's on the interstate

4. Look! I've got a bunch of balloons with my name on them!

3. A girl like you could help a guy forget the irreparable damage he's done to the Republican Party

2. I'll be Vice President after we beat Dukakis and Lloyd Bridges

1. Why, yes, I'm Pat Sajak

TOP TEN LEAST POPULAR ATTRACTIONS AT DISNEY WORLD

10. The Raw Sewage Flume

9. Oprah Mountain

8. Moses Malone's Enchanted Laundry Hamper

7. Parade of short actors in stifling animal suits

6. Pegleg Pete's Prison Shower Room

5. Muggyland

4. Hall of Vice Presidents

3. Walt's Walk-in Freezer and Crypt

2. Turn the Hose on Lady and the Tramp

1. Peter Pan's All-Male Cinema

THE EASTER BUNNY'S TOP TEN PET PEEVES

10. Having to cross I-95

9. Being mistaken for Shelley Duvall

8. Hopping induces vertigo

7. All the red tape involved in getting a liquor license

6. Finding out your date is just a furry pink house slipper

5. Can't we get someone bigger than Bob Barker as an anti-fur spokesman?

4. Drunken calls from Santa reminding you the kids *really* love him

3. When the Gambinos won't give you a lousy extra week to come up with the cash

2. Jewish kids who own BB guns

1. Ticks in your fur the size of jelly beans

TOP TEN LEAST-USED
HYPHENATED WORDS

10. Lick-proof

9. Owl-flavored

8. Hat-resistant

7. Trunk-ripened

6. Gumbel-scented

5. Post-moistened

4. Hitler-riffic

3. Casket-tested

2. Pants-happy

1. Mookie-proofed

TOP TEN SLOGANS FOR CHER'S NEW PERFUME

10. I Smell You, Babe

9. It's Like Having a Tattoo in a Bottle

8. I'm Not Gonna Pay a Lot for This Perfume!

7. It's Cher-riffic!

6. The Crowning Touch to Excessive Plastic Surgery

5. It's Easier than Bathing

4. I Get 12 Cents for Every Bottle Sold

3. Now Any Middle-aged Woman Can Marry a Teenager

2. Easy-Pour Splatter-Proof Bottle

1. Bring Out the Bono in Your Man

TOP TEN DONAHUE TOPICS IF DOGS RAN THE SHOW

10. Worm Pill Addicts

9. Dogs Who Use Cat Doors

8. Post-neutering Depression

7. Lady Mud Wrestlers (Well, they're not going to change *everything* about the show)

6. Korea: The Evil Empire

5. Those Romantic Pocono Tick Baths

4. Falling in Love with Your Vet

3. Owners Who Eat *Your* Leftovers

2. Why Quayle?

1. When to Stop Licking Yourself

TOP TEN LEAST POPULAR PEPPERIDGE FARM COOKIES

10. Asbestos Snaps

9. Broccoloons

8. Tainted Oyster Dainties

7. Gravel Sandys

6. Cinnamon Sharptons

5. Cholesterol Chubbies

4. Spackle Swirlies

3. Mallomar Khaddafys

2. Monkey Clumps

1. Johnny Bench's Nut Cups

TOP TEN LEAST-LOVED CHRISTMAS STORIES

10. Amahl and the Gorgeous Ladies of Wrestling

9. The Sweatiest Angel

8. Santa's Three-Day Eggnog Bender

7. Christmas Eve at the All-Male Cinema

6. A Holiday Visit from Salmonella

5. Ironman Mike Tyson Hurts Santa Real Bad

4. My Christmas Sauna with Burl Ives

3. Jack Frost Loses the Feeling in His Extremities

2. I Saw Daddy Kissing Santa Claus

1. The Teddy Bear Who Came to Life and Mauled a Retail Clerk

TOP TEN SUMMER JOBS
IN HELL

10. Intestine adjuster

9. Professional bowler chaperone

8. Pit bull tickler

7. Rex Reed's living chair

6. Cleveland Indians ticket scalper

5. Personal scratcher to Mr. Ed Asner

4. Understudy to big Kool-Aid pitcher

3. Hornet groomer

2. Staff psychologist, Islamic Jihad

1. Human axle, Raymond Burr's town car

TOP TEN DUTIES OF THE NEW JAPANESE EMPEROR

10. Validate parking for world leaders who stayed more than 2 hours at funeral

9. Impress U.N. General Assembly by slicing tin can with Ginsu knife

8. Call Dan Quayle at 3 in the morning and scream *"Banzai!"* into phone

7. Record "Your lights are on" for use in all talking Toyotas

6. Befriend Pat Morita; find out who's gay in Hollywood

5. Organize title fight between Mike Tyson and Mothra

4. Find "friends" for John Tower when he's in town

3. See that Yoko Ono's U.S. citizenship is kept up-to-date

2. Defend crown every 6 months as required by World Wrestling Federation bylaws

1. Make sure America isn't late with the rent check

TOP TEN LEAST POPULAR
BROADWAY SHOWS

10. *Oprah-homa!*

9. *Sunday in the Park with George Steinbrenner*

8. *Twelve Angry Men and a Baby*

7. *Sharptonmania*

6. *Roy Rogers' Incontinent Dog and Monkey Rodeo*

5. *I'm Not Gonna Pay a Lot for This Muffler: A Dramatic Reading by James Earl Jones*

4. *David Brinkley's Enchanted World of Magic and Illusion*

3. *Meese!*

2. *Death of an Amway Salesman*

1. *Oh! Velveeta!*

TOP TEN TERRIFYING THOUGHTS THAT COME TO YOU AS YOU'RE FALLING ASLEEP

10. What if there are *other* Stallone brothers?

9. That guy moving in next door sure looked a lot like Jon "Bowser" Bauman.

8. Could I get a rash on the *inside* of my skin?

7. Did I really give Wendell my home number?

6. What if God is a lot like Howie Mandel?

5. I could've *sworn* I saw Jimmy the Greek behind the hamper!

4. What if the musical <u>Cats</u> *is* now and forever?

3. Is that *my* hand?

2. What the hell is in secret sauce?

1. What if John Gotti didn't think I was kidding?

TOP TEN THINGS HEARD AT THE ST. PATRICK'S DAY PARADE

10. "Today, my name is Mayor O'Koch."

9. "All right! *Another* bagpipe band."

8. "Gee, food sure tastes good when you boil it."

7. "You have the right to remain silent . . ."

6. "That's not a float—that's Tip O'Neill."

5. "Aww . . . not on my shoes!"

4. "These foreign cars tip over much easier."

3. "Hey, that guy's not wearing green—kill him!"

2. "While we're in the neighborhood, let's drop by the Museum of Modern Art."

1. "You'll get your personal effects back downtown, Monsignor."

TOP TEN THINGS LINCOLN WOULD SAY IF HE WERE ALIVE TODAY

10. "Through the years, the Union has been preserved."

9. "We still must strive to reach our goal of equality."

8. "How much money do I get from these Lincoln Logs?"

7. "I really like the taste of menthol cigarettes."

6. "What the hell is Donahue doing in Russia?"

5. "Why is the video store always out of *Mandingo*?"

4. "I really think I should have been the king in that Civil War chess set."

3. "Hey, babe, that's me on the five-dollar bill."

2. "Eeaagh! Iron bird!"

1. "That fruit Jefferson gets Monticello. I get a tunnel."

TOP TEN THINGS OVERHEARD AT NEW YORK CITY PAY PHONES

10. "Nine-One-One? . . . Sure, I'll Hold."

9. "Ooh. What's this goo on the earpiece?"

8. "Mr. Gotti, that 'leaky pipe' won't be bothering you anymore."

7. "It's a pushbutton phone, but I didn't use my fingers."

6. "This is Elvis. Any messages for me?"

5. "You don't know me, but your number spells out O-BITE-ME."

4. "This is Frank Stallone. I'm calling from my—uh—car phone."

3. "Gotta run—Don't want to miss a single minute of the Summer Olympic coverage broadcast September fifteenth to October fourth—only on NBC!"

2. "Is that a thumb in the coin return?"

1. "Hello. Al Sharpton's office."

TOP TEN SUMMER SAFETY TIPS FROM JIMMY "THE WEASEL" FRATIANNO

10. In Italian restaurants, only order food to go

9. Wait one hour after eating before getting thrown in East River

8. No horseplay while swinging on a meathook

7. To avoid dehydration, drink plenty of fluids before being locked in a trunk

6. Always grasp knife by handle when removing it from between your ribs

5. Always fasten your seat belt, even in a car compactor

4. When being held underwater, don't let flailing arms knock radio into tub

3. Don't be seen having brunch with Geraldo Rivera (good advice for anybody)

2. To avoid accidents at home, remember: Drapes don't have shoes

1. Call Triple A to start your car in the event you want to start it

CAMPBELL'S TOP TEN LEAST POPULAR SOUPS

10. Cream of Gristle

9. Tomato Garagiola

8. Old-fashioned Grease and Weasel

7. Mink Bisque

6. Turkey with Platformate

5. Tap Water and Lawn Trimmings

4. Turkish Prison Surprise

3. Bryant Gumbo

2. Sideburns 'N' Barley

1. Manhattan-Style Windex and Shrimp

TOP TEN THINGS OVERHEARD AT A SENIOR LEAGUE BASEBALL GAME

10. "Is that a signal or is he adjusting his truss?"

9. "A correction for you home viewers— that was *not* in slo-mo."

8. "Are those pinstripes or varicose veins?"

7. "Wow! The wind really got under that hairpiece!"

6. "That's not Morgana! That's Bea Arthur!"

5. "I'll bet he *does* live through the game, Mr. Rose."

4. "You wanna wake the guy in the on-deck circle?"

3. "Hey, batter! Hey, batter! . . . Uh, I forgot what I was going to say."

2. "Oatmeal! Get your nice hot oatmeal!"

1. "Have you ever smelled so much Ben-Gay?"

TOP TEN THINGS
OVERHEARD AT THE
BERLIN WALL

10. "I came for the political freedom—I'm staying for the McRibs!"

9. "Is this the line for Batman?"

8. "So many Benettons!"

7. "As long as you're already in the trunk, let's go to a drive-in."

6. "We're coming to save you, Zsa Zsa!"

5. "Here in the West, we don't have to pay a lot for our muffler."

4. "Finally I can realize my lifelong dream of attending a taping of the PTL Club."

3. "Let's stay at Dave's house!"

2. "This ought to scare the crap out of the French."

1. "We're going to Disney World."

TOP TEN THINGS OVERHEARD AT THE ROCK AND ROLL HALL OF FAME INDUCTION CEREMONY

10. "Pleased to meet you, Bo. Is this *Mrs.* Diddley?"

9. "How was the food at the Betty Ford Center?"

8. "How come nobody's sitting with Albert Goldman?"

7. "The Archies haven't been the same since Jughead died."

6. "David Crosby wants to know if you're gonna finish your dessert."

5. "I'm sorry, Mr. Yastrzemski, but you're at the wrong banquet."

4. "Keith is such a healthy blue color."

3. "Sure the pay is good, but working with Letterman every night really sucks."

2. "Could you please lift your head out of my salad?"

1. "May I see some I.D., Mr. Presley?"

TOP TEN LINES FROM THE NEW *STAR TREK* MOVIE

10. Captain! There's a horrible life form on your head! Oh, sorry. It's your hairpiece.

9. Surprise! Those aren't dilithium crystals—they're Folgers crystals!

8. Damn it, Jim! I'm a doctor—not a very good actor!

7. Don't let Kirk show you what he calls "the Captain's log."

6. Computer analysis of the tape indicates it really is Rob Lowe.

5. Geez—I'm sick of you guys!

4. It's been a century since they changed your planet's name from Earth to Trump.

3. Oh, yeah? Well, beam *this* up, pal!

2. What the hell is Don King doing here?

1. Screw the Final Frontier! Let's go see *Batman*.

TOP TEN THINGS OVERHEARD IN A G.E. RESEARCH LAB

10. "Wow! Look at that stuff burn!"

9. "I keep forgetting which is AC and which is DC."

8. "Are you crazy? Do you know how much a recall would cost?"

7. "Whoops!"

6. "Watch what happens when I toss these bolts into the turbine."

5. "Hey! I think this is the episode where they almost get off the island!"

4. "What we save on the radiation shield, we can put into advertising."

3. "The new guy developed a new long-lasting inexpensive filament. Kill him."

2. "The squid is no longer responding to the mind control! Aaiieeeeee!"

1. "Here comes the tour group. Put your pants on."

TOP TEN OTHER THREATS GOD MADE TO ORAL ROBERTS

10. Send him Redd Foxx as a houseguest

9. Make him die-hard Seattle Mariners fan

8. Force him to spend lots of his free time with Judd Nelson

7. Have the figures on his Civil War chess set come alive and make fun of his clothing

6. Give Fred "The Hammer" Williamson the power to strip-search him at any time

5. Force him to lend pocket comb to Jerry Lewis

4. Pepper his speech with "okie-dokies"

3. Disturb his sleep with 3 A.M. phone calls from a teary-eyed Larry King

2. Take all black players off the Oral Roberts University basketball team

1. Make him spend eternity in a Bonanza Steakhouse with Carol Channing

TOP TEN QUESTIONS ASKED ON THE NBC TOUR

10. Who plays the part of Tom Brokaw on the Nightly News?

9. Are all those rats for a show?

8. Can I slap Gene Shalit?

7. Why do we have to wear goggles around the "Today" show set?

6. How art thou, brother? (Quakers only)

5. When do we get to the shark?

4. Why can't people live in peace together?

3. Does Roger Mudd give *every* tour the finger?

2. Can I have my money back?

1. Whaddya mean—Cosby's in Brooklyn?

TOP TEN THINGS SHIRLEY MacLAINE WAS IN PREVIOUS LIVES

10. George Washington's special friend Howie

9. Original Darren on "Bewitched"

8. Big dumb fish (mid-thirteenth century)

7. Confucius groupie

6. Equipment manager, Buffalo Sabers

5. Undercooked chop sent back by President Wilson

4. Another big dumb fish (late sixteenth century)

3. Lieutenant Colonel Henry Blake on "M.A.S.H." (Oops, I'm sorry, that's McLean Stevenson)

2. Plankton eaten by big dumb fish (early nineteenth century)

1. Can of Stop 'N' Shop diagonally sliced green beans

TOP TEN THINGS COMMUNISTS ARE NO DAMN GOOD AT

10. Surfing

9. Imitating Elvis

8. Laying rubber in front of the Dairy Queen

7. Arena football

6. Stage-diving at Motorhead concerts

5. Broadcasting warm sitcoms featuring lovable black families

4. Naming soft ice cream cakes

3. Ball-scuffing

2. Producing a boxer with as much heart as Rocky

1. Guessing Final Jeopardy

TOP TEN THINGS THAT WILL GET YOU KICKED OUT OF DISNEY WORLD

10. Driving down Main Street U.S.A. with Bambi's mother strapped to your fender

9. Dumping medical waste into Sleeping Beauty's moat

8. Boarding the monorail and announcing you're Bernie Goetz

7. Taunting the guy in the Pluto costume for not being able to get a better job

6. Declaring loudly, "I *do* believe in Tinkerbell" in the men's room

5. Going after Chip and Dale with a weed-whacker

4. After biting into snack bar sandwich saying, "I taste mouse"

3. Taking a leak in the Enchanted Forest

2. Parading around in "Home of the Matterhorn" underwear

1. Bringing your own mouse suit

A group of Canadian high prelates, headed by Paul Emile Cardinal Leger *(center right)*, Archbishop of Montreal, poses in front of Saint Peter's Basilica in 1962. *(AP/Wide World Photos)*

Grand Coulee Dam *(UPI/Bettmann)*

Immigrants passing through the depot at Ellis Island. The peak of the mass movement for immigration was reached in 1907 when 1,285,349 were admitted, over a million of whom entered by way of New York. *(UPI/ Bettmann)*

View of Cairo, Egypt, looking across the "City of the Dead," toward the far hills *(AP/Wide World Photos)*

Two of the famous nineteenth-century orators who played major roles in the development of our democratic nation were Henry Clay *(left)*, who crafted the Missouri Compromise, and Massachusetts' Daniel Webster *(right)*. *(Photo courtesy of Library of Congress)*

Fremont Street, Las Vegas, looking east, circa 1932 *(Las Vegas News Bureau)*

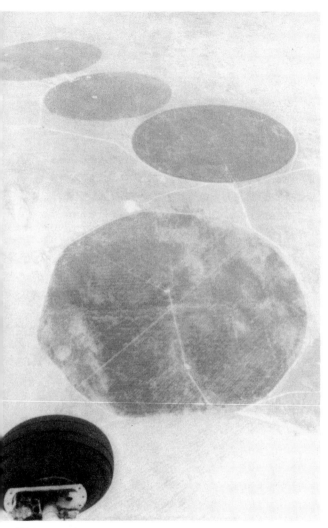

This aerial view depicts a center pivot irrigation system which leaves the soil dark where it's watered in the dry fields of western Nebraska. Lower left corner is the wheel of an airplane. *(AP/Wide World Photos)*

President Truman holds up for the benefit of the throng that turned out to greet him at St. Louis's Union Station, November 4, 1948, a copy of the *Chicago Tribune,* published early election night with the headline "Dewey Defeats Truman." *(St. Louis Mercantile Library Association)*

The landing of Commodore Matthew C. Perry of the U.S. Navy at Uraga on the shore of Tokyo Bay in 1853. Japan had been shut off from the rest of the world by its military rulers. Perry's landing paved the way for the first treaty of amity and commerce between Japan and the U.S. *(AP/Wide World Photos)*

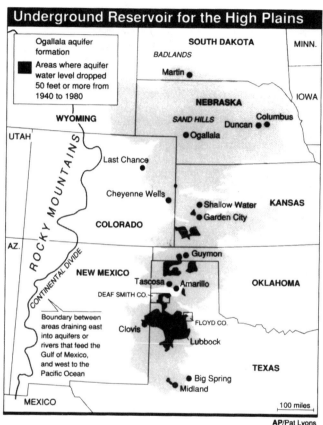

Underground Reservoir for the High Plains

Ogallala aquifer formation

Areas where aquifer water level dropped 50 feet or more from 1940 to 1980

SOUTH DAKOTA

MINN.

BADLANDS

Martin

IOWA

NEBRASKA

WYOMING

SAND HILLS

Duncan Columbus

UTAH

Ogallala

R
O
C
K
Y

M
O
U
N
T
A
I
N
S

Last Chance

Cheyenne Wells

COLORADO

Shallow Water

Garden City

KANSAS

CONTINENTAL DIVIDE

AZ.

Guymon

NEW MEXICO

Tascosa

Amarillo

OKLAHOMA

DEAF SMITH CO.

Boundary between areas draining east into aquifers or rivers that feed the Gulf of Mexico, and west to the Pacific Ocean

Clovis

FLOYD CO.

Lubbock

Big Spring

Midland

TEXAS

MEXICO

100 miles

AP/Pat Lyons

(AP/Wide World Photos)

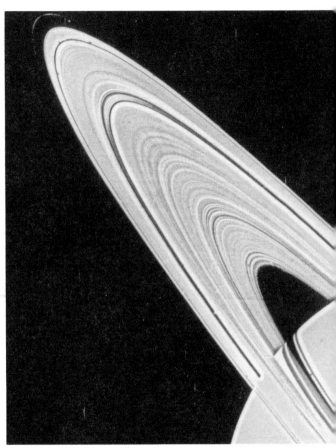

Computer-assembled two-image mosaic of Saturn's rings, taken by NASA's Voyager I on November 6, 1980, at a range of 8 million kilometers (5 million miles), showing approximately 95 individual concentric features in the rings. *(UPI/Bettmann)*

TOM BROKAW'S TOP TEN TURN-ONS

10. Long walks on the beach

9. A perfumed bath on a rainy afternoon

8. Raisa Gorbachev in a waitress uniform

7. Doing the news with no pants on

6. When they sneak some swear words into a PG movie

5. Connie Chung's discarded makeup sponges

4. Slow dancing in the White House briefing room

3. Body glitter

2. Hang-gliding nude over state prisons

1. Fat checkout girls who wear a ton of makeup

TOP TEN UNPLEASANT THINGS TO HEAR ON AN ELEVATOR

10. Does this look infected to you?

9. Do you know these pants are reversible?

8. Hold the door! Willard's coming!

7. The acoustics in this elevator are perfect for yodeling.

6. Sorry about my finger. I was aiming for a button.

5. Would you do a number for us, Miss Channing?

4. We're both going to the fourteenth floor. How about a hug?

3. I'm not just a Jehovah's Witness—I also sell insurance.

2. Does this smell like root beer to you?

1. Just ignore Duke. We're going to have him fixed soon.

TOP TEN WAYS AMERICAN CARS WOULD BE DIFFERENT IF RALPH NADER HAD NEVER BEEN BORN

10. Dashboard hibachis

9. Seat belts made of piano wire

8. Windshield replaced with ant farm for the kids

7. Strobe headlights make oncoming traffic look like old-time movie

6. 50-foot antennas allow you to broadcast while driving

5. Optional front-seat hammocks

4. Wiper fluid reservoir routinely filled with Thousand Island dressing

3. New York City taxis would be exactly the same

2. The paper Buick

1. Speedometer replaced with electronic voice chanting "Punch it! Punch it!"

TOP TEN REASONS
HUGH HEFNER WILL MAKE
A GOOD FATHER

10. Can warm bottles of formula in the hot tub

9. Could teach child math while explaining how his half sister is older than his mother

8. No greater authority figure than a dad who hangs around all day in a bathrobe

7. Jimmy Caan always available to babysit

6. Can help them make college choice through a "Girls of the Big Ten" pictorial

5. If kid gets flu, there's plenty of penicillin on hand

4. Could lull tot to sleep with nursery rhyme about "The Man from Nantucket"

3. Can teach youngster the facts of life using nude photos of Mom

2. Hef would make the swingingest Little League coach ever

1. If he didn't care about America's young people, he wouldn't marry them

TOP TEN REJECTED CIRCUS SLOGANS

10. Catch clown fever!

9. Come smell the excitement!

8. Yes! We have middle-aged women in spangled bikinis!

7. Don't wear shoes you care about.

6. The lowest-paid performers on earth —we pass the savings on to you!

5. Our clowns have all their shots!

4. No shirt. No shoes. No problem!

3. Come see us before the immigration department does!

2. Ever see camels do it?

1. Come have a corndog with the human torso!

TOP TEN WAYS LAS VEGAS IS BETTER THAN PARIS

10. Vegas not crawling with Frenchmen

9. Impossible to get "I Crapped Out in Paris" T-shirts

8. Hard to get change in Louvre at 4 A.M.

7. Paris inconveniently located thousands of miles from nuclear test sites

6. Sorbonne basketball team is five tiny white guys

5. Paris: men in berets on bicycles. Las Vegas: orangutans in cowboy hats on unicycles

4. Vegas didn't lose a single inch of ground to Nazi war machine

3. Palace of Versailles does not offer double jackpot time every 15 minutes

2. Ten dollars won't buy you sex act in desert outside Paris

1. Las Vegans: hardworking, patriotic citizens. Parisians: lazy, wine-swilling cheeseheads

TOP TEN DONALD TRUMP PICKUP LINES

10. How'd you like to be a *New York Post* headline?

9. Haven't I evicted you somewhere before?

8. You don't know Marvin Mitchelson, do you?

7. Care to take a ride on the Trump Shuttle?

6. I'd like to do to you what I did to Merv

5. I can introduce you to Don King

4. Hello. I'm Donald Trump

3. Tired of always running to the automated cash machine?

2. I'm good friends with Dave Letterman

1. That *is* a roll of hundreds in my pocket —*and* I'm glad to see you

TOP TEN WAYS LIFE WOULD BE DIFFERENT IF DOGS RAN THE WORLD

10. More Donahue shows about shedding

9. Presidential candidates more likely to stop in mid-speech and sniff base of podium

8. Cats must report address to post office every year

7. Procter and Gamble introduces new liver-flavored Crest

6. Drinking from toilet no longer a faux pas

5. Museums filled with still lifes of table scraps

4. Constitutional amendment extends vote to wolves

3. TV commercial altered so dog catches and devours little chuckwagon

2. Monument in Washington commemorates "Our Neutered Brothers"

1. All motorists must drive with head out of car window

TOP TEN WAYS THE DALAI LAMA WILL SPEND HIS NOBEL PRIZE MONEY

10. Get saxophone out of hock

9. No more "budget" English muffins

8. Give Cadillacs to Sonny and Red

7. New kitchen cabinets for Mrs. Lama

6. Give it to Pete Rose; see if he can double it

5. Bail out Merv Griffin

4. Put finishing touches on Lamaland Amusement Park

3. Kegger!

2. Hush money to former temple secretary

1. One seriously large order of McDonald's french fries

TOP TEN WAYS DAN RATHER COULD CONCLUDE "THE CBS EVENING NEWS"

10. Put finger in cheek; make cork-popping sound

9. Pretend to "sweep up" spotlight on floor

8. Say "Nighty-night" and put head on desk

7. Reveal which news story of the evening was the fake one

6. Lick lips and say, "Mmm-mmm, time for pie!"

5. Give coded message to "Li'l Newshounds" fan club

4. Wink and say, "Pour the gin, Lydia, I'm on my way home."

3. Hurl sweat-soaked scarf to female fans

2. Light big cigar and say, "Ha-ha! See you tomorrow, suckers!"

1. Feed carrot to CBS News bunny

TOP TEN WAYS TO ADD EXCITEMENT TO A LONG CAR TRIP

10. Play "auto-bingo"

9. Try to eat ear of corn while steering

8. Play connect-the-dots with dead bugs on windshield

7. Practice sudden bootlegger turns

6. When traffic is light, drop pants around your ankles

5. Have long conversations with imaginary friends after picking up hitchhikers

4. Lean on horn and swerve as you approach stalled motorists

3. Tune to static on radio and pretend you're the last person on earth

2. See how long you can drive with your eyes closed

1. Talk guy behind counter at Stuckey's into leaving family and joining you

TOP TEN REJECTED
DONAHUE TOPICS

10. People who keep thinking it's Tuesday

9. Heterosexual men who worship Judy Garland

8. Problems of guys named Don

7. People who have seen Raymond Burr naked

6. Blacks who really get a kick out of Sonny Bono

5. Department store Santas who marry their customers

4. People who swear Rex Reed stares in their windows at night

3. Invisible mute people who don't show up on videotape

2. Women who just can't forget Ted Bessell

1. Professional bowlers who touch themselves

TOP TEN WAYS TO MAKE GEORGE BUSH MORE EXCITING

10. Kill a man with his bare hands on network TV

9. Divorce Barbara; marry 13-year-old cousin

8. Stick his tongue in Sam Donaldson's ear during press conference

7. Disappear into Alaskan wilderness with Rosanna Arquette; return with necklace made of bear teeth

6. Change campaign slogan from "Bush in '88" to "Party with the Bushmeister"

5. Answer questions on "Meet the Press" with "I'm too drunk to remember"

4. Have him bend standing microphone into pretzel shape; give to cub reporter as souvenir

3. Nickname him George "the sexecutioner" Bush

2. Start hanging with Earth, Wind and Fire

1. Shorter speeches, tighter pants

TOP TEN BODY PARTS OR VAN PATTENS

10. Heart

9. Kidney

8. Vincent

7. Trachea

6. Joyce

5. James

4. Bladder

3. Timothy

2. Spleen

1. Dick

TOP TEN WAYS PEOPLE PRONOUNCE "BOLOGNA"

10. Balogna (Ba Lo Nah)

9. Baloney (Ba Lo Nee)

8. Balonia (Ba Lo Nya)

7. Ballooning (Ba Lun Ing)

6. Fellini (Fe Lee Nee)

5. Abalone (A Buh Lo Nee)

4. Papillon (Pa Pee Yon)

3. Aloney-bae (Uh Lo Nee Bay)

2. Bloney (Blo Nee)

1. Bumoney (Buh Mo Nee)

TOP TEN WAYS TO MAKE COMMUNISM FUN AGAIN

10. Spell it with a "K."

9. Have Castro do guest shot on "Cosby"

8. Add mechanical shark attraction at Lenin's tomb

7. Have Revlon introduce new "Khmer Rouge"

6. Give everybody red birthmark decals to wear on forehead

5. Adopt "Lovable Loser" persona—like the '61 Mets

4. Get Skip Gorbachev to do a "Not Your Father's Oldsmobile" commercial

3. Hire "The Chicken" to disrupt Politburo meetings

2. Have Deng Xiaopeng cry during Barbara Walters interview

1. Less centralized economic planning; more rock

YASIR ARAFAT'S TOP TEN WAYS TO IMPROVE THE PLO'S IMAGE

10. Award frequent flyer mileage during hijackings

9. Pass out marshmallows at firebombings

8. Have Itzhak Perlman over for a nice piece of fish

7. Put really funny message on office answering machine

6. Change name to "Palestinian Good Olds Guys"

5. Promise that for every airport bombing, we'll donate 50 cents to the Sierra Club

4. Kidnap Geraldo. Keep him

3. Expell Jim and Tammy from ministry; freeze their assets (I'm sorry, that's how to improve the *PTL*'s image)

2. Lots of Binaca

1. New slogan: "You're never fully dressed without a smile"

MIKE TYSON'S TOP TEN WAYS TO MEND A BROKEN HEART

10. Take a warm bath, sip a fine brandy and toss a sofa through a plate-glass window

9. Spend week trout-fishing with Don King

8. Compare your own life with Leon Spinks'

7. Float rose petals in your spit bucket

6. Put on as much gold jewelry as your spine can withstand

5. Remember: There are plenty of heartless, calculating gold diggers in the sea

4. Remind yourself that your best years as a casino-greeter lie ahead

3. Rush into a hasty marriage with Brigitte Nielsen

2. Pictionary, Pictionary, Pictionary!

1. Try to see the good in each new mother/daughter team you go out with

TOP TEN UNSAFE TOYS FOR CHRISTMAS

10. Junior Electrician Outlet Patrol

9. Hasbro's Slippery Steps

8. Black & Decker Silly Driller

7. Roof Hanger Paratrooper Outfit

6. Remco's Pocket Hive

5. Traffic Tag

4. Will It Burn? From Parker Brothers

3. Chimney Explorer

2. My First Ferret Farm

1. Ooh—You're Blue!, the Hold-Your-Breath Game

TOP TEN SIGNS THAT YOU'RE REALLY IN LOVE WITH TOM BROKAW

10. You hear Tom's voice, even when the news isn't on

9. You think the new Whitney Houston song was written just for you and Tom

8. Your picture of Dan Rather suddenly seems so childish

7. You get a queasy feeling when he jokes with Connie Chung

6. You daydream about him working on his car with his shirt off

5. You pray for international catastrophes so there will be more special reports

4. Your license plate is "LUVTOM"

3. You have videocassettes of his three MGM musicals from the '50s

2. You snatch his clothes from the laundromat dryer

1. You derail Amtrak trains to get his attention

TOP TEN NAMES FOR ROBERT BORK'S BEARD

10. The Chin Slinky

9. The Amish Outlaw

8. The See-Through

7. My Very First Beard—from Kenner!

6. The Lunatic Fringe

5. Señor Itchy

4. The Radioactive Goat

3. Salute to C. Everett Koop

2. Gopher Butt

1. The Babe Magnet

TOP TEN NUMBERS
BETWEEN ONE AND TEN

10. Seven

9. Four

8. Ten

7. Three

6. Eight and a half

5. Nine

4. Two

3. One

2. Eight

1. Five and Six   *(tie)*

TOP TEN PAPERS WRITTEN BY BROOKE SHIELDS AT PRINCETON

10. William Shakespeare: His Poetry Rates a Ten

9. A Chemical Process in Three Stages: Lather, Rinse, Repeat

8. Girls with Thin Eyebrows: Hideous Freaks of Nature

7. Cliff Notes Versus Monarch Notes: Two Views of *Hamlet*

6. Circles, Flowers, a Smiling Guy: So Many Ways to Dot the "I"

5. The Pushy Overbearing Mother Figure in Literature

4. Pretty Leaves I Found Outside Somewhere

3. Black Americans: What I Hope to Say When I Meet One

2. Philosophy: Why Don't They Spell It with an "F"?

1. The Male Organ: What It Might Look Like

TOP TEN PROM THEMES

10. We Remember Khomeini

9. Our Sagging Dollar

8. A Night in Drew Barrymore's Basement

7. Mudslide!

6. The Best Years of Our Lives Are Now Over

5. Satanic Teenage Time Bombs

4. Surrounded by Infected Ticks

3. Our Crummy Gym with a Couple of Streamers

2. Rob Lowe Pajama Party

1. McDonald's Is Hiring

TOP TEN PUNCH LINES TO SCOTTISH DIRTY JOKES

10. It took me a fortnight to get out the thistles

9. I didn't know you could also get wool from them!

8. It's not a bagpipe, but don't stop playing

7. What made you think I was talking about golf?

6. I've heard of comin' through the rye—but this is ridiculous!

5. Of course she's served millions—she's a McDonald

4. Oh, so *you're* Wade Boggs

3. Care to shake hands with the Loch Ness monster?

2. Who's burning argyles?

1. She's in the distillery making Johnnie Walker Red

TOP TEN QUESTIONS ASKED ON THE WHITE HOUSE TOUR

10. Can I crash here tonight?

9. What number president was Martin Sheen?

8. Hey, cool! Whose slot cars?

7. When will we reach Elvis' final resting place?

6. How can George Bush *stand* her?

5. Can a man really be in love with two women at the same time?

4. Why are your hamburgers square? (Oops, that's the White *Castle* tour)

3. When's the next showing of *Captain Eo*?

2. Are you cooking beans?

1. Wow! Who's the blonde with Weinberger?

TOP TEN NAMES FOR THE LETTERMAN ESTATE

10. Camp David

9. Graceland North

8. Drifter's Haven

7. The Old Helmsley Place

6. Colonel Dave's Post World War III Love Bunker

5. The Deep Woods Tick Ranch

4. The Taj Mahal Gurnee

3. The House that Ruth Buzzi Built

2. The Swankienda

1. Shangri-Dave

TOP TEN QUESTIONS
SCIENCE CANNOT ANSWER

10. Which one's Kate and which one's Allie?

9. How did Ed McMahon get my home address?

8. How can those guys on the street sell real Rolexes for ten bucks?

7. Why don't the laws of physics inhibit the expansion of Paul Prudhomme?

6. How can those wrestling refs miss so many illegal holds?

5. How could the IRS be so dense about my so-called "church"?

4. Why do men achieve orgasm in a second while women never have them?

3. Why, if Mr. Ed could talk, did he never complain about having to stand in straw soaked in his own urine?

2. How can a list of ten short items seem to take an hour to read?

1. What exactly was Jimmy the Greek bred for?

TOP TEN RASTA EXPRESSIONS OR BASEBALL CHATTER

10. Hey batter, hey batter

9. Him a natty dread mon

8. Lively up yourself

7. No batter, no batter

6. Easy out

5. Ride, natty, ride

4. Stick it in his ear

3. Hungry mon is an angry mon

2. Make him pitch to ya

1. Easy skanking/Hum babe   *(tie)*

TOP TEN REASONS
AL SHARPTON AND I
ARE BEST FRIENDS

10. He gives me a good deal on Lionel Richie tickets

9. I call him "reverend" and he calls me "admiral"

8. Together we form the best two-man beach volleyball team on the East Coast

7. We're collaborating on a book of children's stories

6. The more he's in the news, the less attention paid to my messy divorce from Julianne Phillips

5. Gave me my street name "Dave"

4. Has my likeness on his gold medallion

3. Usually volunteers to get in trunk when we go to the drive-in

2. Most of the time, neither of us knows what we're talking about

1. He makes my haircut look good

TOP TEN THINGS WE AS AMERICANS CAN BE PROUD OF

10. Attendance at Liza Minnelli concerts still optional

9. Greatest number of citizens who have actually boarded UFOs

8. Many newspapers feature "Jumble," that scrambled word game

7. Crumbling landmarks torn down—not made a big fuss over

6. Hourly motel rates

5. Vast majority of Elvis movies made here

4. Didn't just give up right away in World War II like some countries we could mention

3. Goatees and vandykes thought to be worn only by weenies

2. Our well-behaved golf professionals

1. Fabulous babes coast to coast

TOP TEN REASONS
CONGRESS DESERVES
A PAY HIKE

10. Many big corporations cutting back on bribes

9. Because of C-Span, they all had to buy hairpieces

8. Tired of carpooling with Barney Frank

7. Tired of Congressman Fred Grandy's taunts about all the dough he's making from "Love Boat" reruns

6. Most of D.C.'s topless bars have raised their cover

5. Our nation's lawmakers ought to make at least a fraction of the annual income of the "Hey, Vern" guy

4. Worked long hours trying to keep down the minimum wage

3. Maybe they'll stop complaining about salaries and start doing something about our nation's oppressive highway speed limits

2. Close to half have never been indicted

1. If raise doesn't go through, have vowed to turn the whole thing over to Quayle

TOP TEN INTERVIEW QUESTIONS ASKED MISS AMERICA CONTESTANTS

10. Which is your favorite dancing raisin?

9. Can you spell your home state without looking at your banner?

8. How does it feel to be the only contestant with a fat butt?

7. How much of your scholarship money have you lost in the slots?

6. If you were stranded on a desert island with a shampoo for oily hair and creme rinse for dry hair—what would you do?

5. Aren't there any other girls in your state?

4. Don't you want to put some ointment on that?

3. Are those real?

2. Don't you have anything better to do?

1. Would you consider teaming up with Miss Teen U.S.A. to fight crime like Batman and Robin?

TOP TEN REASONS TO DISCONTINUE THE TOP TEN LISTS

10. Snide remarks overheard on elevator

9. Pressure from the big money boys

8. Movie deal not materializing

7. Provides grist for Soviet propaganda mill

6. Affiliates near mutiny

5. Pits brother against brother

4. Looks shabby next to "Soup of the Day"

3. Moving plea from Council of Bishops

2. Complaints of drowsiness

1. Angry letter from Lou Rawls

PRINCESS DIANA'S TOP TEN COMPLAINTS ABOUT PRINCE CHARLES

10. Repulsive orange teeth after scarfing down entire bag of Cheetos

9. Threatens me with beheading for leaving nylons hanging in bathroom

8. Giggles like a schoolgirl around Buckingham Palace guards

7. That phony British accent

6. Never puts the cap back on the mango love butter

5. Unfavorably compares cooking of my chef to cooking of his mother's chef

4. Laughs like a hyena at reruns of "The Jeffersons"

3. Always calls Pizza Hut before we've decided on topping we want

2. Constantly slips and calls me "Oprah"

1. Wears "Home of Big Ben" boxer shorts

TOP TEN REASONS TO VOTE

10. The chance to take a deep breath in a high school gymnasium

9. Good practice for voting in TV's "People's Choice" awards

8. Exciting to pretend big red lever is actually power switch to electric chair

7. Free pamphlets!

6. When you finish, Red Cross nurse gives you delicious cookies

5. To keep resident Canadians under control

4. You can shout over closed voting booth curtain, "Hey! Who used up all the conditioner?"

3. So we can thumb our noses at the Mexicans and their king

2. So you'll feel personally involved when new mayor gets hauled off to jail

1. Even though it's never come close to happening in over 200 years, your one vote could make a difference!

TOP TEN REASONS WHY THE U.S. IS BETTER THAN SWITZERLAND

10. Our cheese comes wrapped in individual slices

9. Our army carries foot-long bayonets; their army carries corkscrews and tweezers

8. Swiss heavyweight champion cries like a baby when he gets hit

7. Swiss noontime cuckoo din causes ears to bleed

6. So-called "little girls" in Heidi costumes actually hard-boiled midgets with rap sheets as long as your arm

5. Countdown of Top 40 yodeling hits wears thin around number 20

4. People on Swiss streets routinely get into fistfights over the correct time

3. Swiss steak. 'Nuff said

2. While they were dipping fondue, we were kicking Nazi butt

1. We don't have the word "Switzer" in our name

TOP TEN REASONS WHY TV IS BETTER THAN BOOKS

10. Book readers miss out on K-Tel record offers

9. Can't drive and read at the same time

8. No one ever got a paper cut from Hugh Downs

7. Books ask difficult questions, but don't give away cars or Caribbean cruises for right answers

6. Books written by pasty-skinned geeks; TV full of chesty babes

5. "Soul Train"

4. Learning to work TV set solid training for future astronauts

3. "TV" easier to spell than "book"

2. No fun to dance in your underwear in front of book about Jane Pauley

1. Ralph Waldo Emerson . . . "The Equalizer"! . . . 'Nuff said.

TOP TEN REJECTED NAMES FOR JOAN COLLINS' PERFUME

10. Fleet's in!

9. Who's Frying Eggs?

8. Better than that Crap Linda Evans Is Selling

7. Sixtysomething

6. If Symptoms Persist, Contact Your Doctor

5. Suddenly Exxon!

4. Kennel Cough

3. Joan Collins' Latest Cynical Attempt to Cash in on Her Popularity before the Whole World Gets Sick and Tired of Her Once and for All

2. *Really* Old Spice

1. Next!

TOP TEN REJECTED PROVISIONS OF THE CONSTITUTION

10. President may not use army and navy to get back at guy who beat him up in junior high school

9. Give vote to dogs who "think they're people"

8. When the flag passes, everybody has to open eyes as wide as they can and say "Gollee!"

7. Third House of Congress to be filled by really fat guys

6. If President and Vice President die suddenly, office shall be filled by *People* magazine's "Sexiest Man Alive"

5. Cruel and unusual punishment is okay on Andy Rooney

4. The national bird must be served on a bun, never on a stick

3. Each state will have the right to claim they have hottest-looking babes

2. Damage deposit of $25 required before renting White House for keg parties

1. The President can change his last name as often as he likes

TOP TEN ROB LOWE
PICKUP LINES

10. I promise I won't sing

9. BETA or VHS?

8. I was on HBO forty times last month

7. I'm a thinking man's Matt Dillon

6. How'd you like to get on that Maury Povich show?

5. What a coincidence! You want to be an actress and I have a video camera!

4. Care to slip into this Snow White costume?

3. Would you describe your mother as "litigious"?

2. Don't worry. It'll be like the rest of my movies—nobody will see it

1. Why—you're as pretty as I am!

TOP TEN SIGNS THAT CHEF BOY-AR-DEE IS LOSING HIS MIND

10. Believes Spaghetti-Os can be used as birth-control device

9. Obsessed with idea of tomato-based cologne

8. Recently got engaged to Robin Givens

7. Test marketing "Pasta 'N' Thumbs"

6. At recent sales meeting, dropped pants and said, "Let's put the *Boy* back in Boy-ar-dee!"

5. Paranoid delusion that his wife is sleeping with Uncle Ben

4. Every few minutes, and for no apparent reason, yells "Bingo!" at the top of his lungs

3. Believes he is Mrs. David Letterman

2. Instead of traditional chef's "OK" sign, now just gives the finger

1. Taken to splashing himself with spaghetti sauce and wandering through bus station chanting "Lick me"

TOP TEN SIGNS DAN QUAYLE IS GETTING MORE RESPECT

10. Casey Kasem now accepting his calls

 9. Tour groups no longer allowed to use his bathroom

 8. Network news anchors no longer make quotation marks with fingers when they say "The Vice President"

 7. His confidential Secret Service code name now differs from his actual name

 6. No longer gets newspapers *after* the White House puppies

 5. Credibility soared when public found out he wasn't the captain of that Exxon tanker

 4. Gets to use deep end in White House pool

 3. Even *I'm* tired of making jokes about him

 2. People now tell him he's no *Ted* Kennedy

 1. No longer has to wear paper hat saying "Trainee"

TOP TEN SIGNS THAT JOHN HINCKLEY IS MAKING PROGRESS

10. Wrote last letter to Ted Bundy on Snoopy stationery

9. Rewinds tape of *Taxi Driver* before returning it to video store

8. No longer lists occupation as "Crazed Loner" on tax return

7. High-pitched tones in head now play Rodgers & Hammerstein medley

6. Sold line of "Sorry You've been Convicted" cards to Hallmark

5. Has grown out of harmful obsession with Jody Foster, has started one with Foster Brooks

4. Turned down endorsement offer from Doritos

3. Considers himself an "honorary Cosby kid"

2. Booked to play harmonica solo on next "All-Star Salute to Dutch Reagan"

1. Thinks Shirley MacLaine is off her rocker

TOP TEN REJECTED NBA PROMOTIONAL SLOGANS

10. It's Dribble-riffic!

9. A Couple of White Guys Sitting Around the Bench Talking

8. At Least Our Commissioner Isn't Named "Fay"

7. We Hope That Squeaking Sneaker Sound Doesn't Drive You Nuts

6. No George Steinbrenner!

5. Like Big Sweaty Ballerinas

4. Sit Up Close and Smell the Excitement!

3. Unlike Bowling—No Fat Guys

2. Come See Our Johnsons!

1. NBA—We're Easy to Spell!

TOP TEN SIGNS THAT PEOPLE ARE GETTING DUMBER

10. Detailed instructions now provided with all new socks

9. The new Brady Bunch show

8. Nobel Prize for Literature given to guy who first hyphenated "Oat-bran"

7. Quaylemania!

6. Japanese successfully marketing a TV set that's just a cardboard box with a picture of Fess Parker inside it

5. Disney gave me lots of money for movies I have no intention of making

4. Most Americans can name no more than two of the four dancing raisins

3. People will applaud even when no joke has been made

2. Presidential seal now reads, "I'm Not Gonna Pay a Lot for This Muffler"

1. I'm still on the air

TOP TEN GOOD THINGS ABOUT LEONA HELMSLEY

10. Doesn't overburden IRS with large unwieldy tax payments

9. Knows the first name of each of the hundreds of employees she's arbitrarily fired

8. Has remained married for years to same man she stole a fortune from

7. She wept when the Ayatollah passed away

6. Has never swindled Merv Griffin

5. Once slapped an employee so hard it improved his vision

4. At least there's no damn Leona perfume

3. Has delighted millions with hit TV series "The Jeffersons" and "Amen" (Sorry, I was thinking of Sherman Hemsley)

2. Provides inspiring role model for young tax cheats

1. She just happens to be the woman I love

TOP TEN NEW NAMES FOR THE REUNITED GERMANY

10. Keggerland

9. Just Plain Volks

8. Siegfried & Roy

7. Aryan Acres

6. Argentina East

5. The Love Shack

4. Nazichusetts

3. Switzerland's Bad-Ass Neighbor

2. Home of Das Whopper

1. Cindy

TOP TEN COMPLAINTS OF *SPORTS ILLUSTRATED* SWIMSUIT MODELS

10. Skimpy outfits reveal biker tattoos

9. Ever since Paulina Porizkova started dating Ric Ocasek, goofy-looking guys actually think they have a shot with us

8. Knowing your photo is being used as currency in prison

7. Exxon tankers

6. Going on sleazy late-night talk shows where the band leader makes a clumsy pass at you

5. The 1987 Arctic Circle shoot

4. Having to pay cash before pumping your own gas

3. People who mistake your sun protection factor for your I.Q.

2. Creepy feeling that somewhere Jimmy Swaggart is sitting alone looking at a picture of you

1. That damn sand gets in everything

TOP TEN LEAST POPULAR OSCAR MAYER LUNCH MEATS

10. Pulled Hamstring

9. Gristleami

8. Smoked Schwarzenegger

7. Gee, Your Ham Smells Terrific!

6. Eva Braunschweiger

5. San Diego Chicken Roll

4. Joseph Bologna

3. Smokey Pittsburgh Señorita (aimed at Hispanic women smokers who live in the Pittsburgh area)

2. Hey—Those Aren't Pimentos!

1. Hoffaloney

TOP TEN MARION BARRY EXCUSES

10. Went to hotel for the free HBO

9. Used drugs to escape daily nightmare of having first name "Marion"

8. Just helping out Dick and Ed with their nutty "Bloopers and Practical Jokes" show

7. As mayor, has duty to greet visiting foreign dignitaries—you know, like from Colombia

6. President Bush asked him to buy it so he could hold it up during next TV speech

5. Started as craving for those little mints they leave on your pillow—and then just got out of hand

4. Doing what he could to keep drugs out of the hands of our nation's young people

3. Always thought that frying egg in TV drug commercial looked pretty good

2. Drug dealers?! I thought they were prostitutes!

1. If buying crack and getting high in cheap hotel rooms is a crime—why isn't Barbara Bush in jail?

TOP TEN SIGNS THAT SOVIET SOCIETY IS LOOSENING UP

10. Hammer and sickle symbol replaced by smiling Kool-Aid pitcher

9. If Personal Pan Pizza not ready in two minutes, customer no longer beaten senseless

8. Sans-a-Belt slacks

7. Exit visas now available at supermarket checkouts

6. Citizens informed of Elvis' death

5. Call-waiting now offered on tapped phones

4. Shirt and shoe requirement dropped at 7-Eleven

3. Emigrés now presented with lovely parting gifts

2. Bigger and better prizes in *Pravda* Wingo game

1. Bob Eubanks named Grand Marshal of May Day parade

TOP TEN GOOD THINGS
ABOUT A BASEBALL STRIKE

10. San Diego Chicken will be forced to get a real job

9. Gives public time to get used to commissioner named "Fay"

8. Nike can launch ad campaign for "Bo Knows Picket Lines"

7. Chance to round up hundreds of potential Yankees managers

6. It'll be fun to watch Morgana run out to kiss pro bowlers

5. Allows time for that bright orange nacho cheese stuff to really mellow

4. Cleveland fans can boast that Indians are tied for first place

3. Newspapers have more room to devote to Marla Maples

2. Frees up unused Astroturf for my new hairpiece

1. Gives indoor lacrosse a fighting chance

TOP TEN THINGS THE U.S. ARMED FORCES HAVE OVER THE SOVIETS

10. In hand-to-hand combat, U.S. soldier has advantage of having seen professional wrestling

9. Notches on nose of our nuclear missiles make it easier to pop open a beer

8. U.S. Navy pilots go into battle with extra incentive of impressing Kelly McGillis

7. Their geeky haircuts are worse than our geeky haircuts

6. Soviet subs not wired for MTV

5. Our Constitution guarantees the right to say "Bite me" to commanding officer

4. U.S. weapons impeccably constructed by the superefficient Japanese

3. Ivan can't drink Pepsi upside down

2. Less talk, more rock

1. Batman's on *our* side

TOP ELEVEN REJECTED LIFESAVER FLAVORS

11. Disembowelmint

10. Pineapple Noriega

9. Marion-Berry

8. Smouldering Wig

7. Fruit-of-the-Loom

6. Sonny 'N' Cherry

5. Anton Fig

4. Number Ten Steel Lock Washers

3. Suck This

2. Manson Mint

1. Rashberry

TOP TEN RULES OF THE MISS AMERICA PAGEANT

10. Liposuction is permitted, but not as part of the talent competition

9. Contestants must check out of judges' hotel rooms by 11 A.M.

8. Anyone who takes a water break without asking spends a night in the box

7. The balk rule will be enforced

6. Nonfinalists standing in the background may smoke discreetly

5. Scholarship money may not be applied toward candy

4. Contestants with private armies may not topple duly elected winner

3. No Gabors

2. For those who have had cosmetic surgery, at least 80% of their bodies must be from their home state

1. Contestants may use Vaseline on teeth, not on Gary Collins

TOP TEN REJECTED
PROM THEMES

10. Inside the Digestive System

9. Today Is the Yesterday We'll Be Embarrassed about Tomorrow

8. Hormones Ahoy!

7. Stairway to Unrewarding Careers

6. Dorks in Rented Tuxes

5. Restroom Memories

4. Acne! Acne! Acne!

3. Marry Early for a Lifetime of Misery

2. Emergency Room, Here We Come!

1. Geeks-a-Poppin'!

TOP TEN REJECTED
AFTER-SCHOOL SPECIALS

10. The Boy Who Counted Cards

9. Please Don't Make Me Go on "Family Feud"

8. The Day the Gym Teacher Cried

7. The Popular Boy Who Smoked and Drank a Lot

6. Hiking with Reverend Al

5. Never Kiss a Rodeo Clown

4. Nugget, the Golden Retriever with Problem Flatulence

3. Tiffany and Debbie Gibson: The Catfight

2. From Larry Holmes, with Love

1. Father Was a Flight Attendant

TOP TEN FUN THINGS ABOUT BEING MIKHAIL GORBACHEV

10. Using KGB surveillance equipment to get free HBO

9. Can jump turnstile to Moscow subway and nobody says a word

8. Staging fake battle scenes in Afghanistan and then selling the footage to CBS

7. On opening day of Soviet auto show, got to be the first one to sit in the Batmobile

6. Constitutionally empowered to strip-search any citizen

5. The Whammo Company is always sending free stuff

4. Counter guys at Moscow McDonald's usually slip in a couple extra McNuggets

3. Lucrative Jockey underwear endorsement deal

2. Gets to play Santa at end of May Day parades

1. Raisa after two glasses of wine

TOP TEN EXHIBITS IN THE ROCK AND ROLL HALL OF FAME

10. Michael Jackson's original nose

9. Diorama of Pink Floyd trashing a Holiday Inn

8. The Childproof Cap Elvis Couldn't Open

7. The mint green shorts worn by Richard Simmons in "Sweatin' to the Oldies"

6. The Life of Mark Goodman: From MTV Veejay to Former MTV Veejay

5. The Record Company Weasel Petting Zoo

4. Great Moments with Mister Mister

3. Get the Hell Off the Stage!: A Tribute to Opening Acts

2. "Catch a Disease from a Groupie" kissing booth

1. Ride the Wild Cher

MRS. NORIEGA'S TOP TEN PET PEEVES

10. Clearasil on pillowcases

9. Every Thursday, it's torture night with the boys

8. He keeps track of big bundles of drug money but can't remember the last time he paid the paper boy

7. Husbands who violently threaten the U.S.A. just when you're about to fly to New York to catch Tyne Daly in *Gypsy*

6. Kids who don't want to get up from in front of the TV when you ask them to carry a sack of cocaine out to the Cessna

5. Every anniversary the same thing: Banana Republic gift certificates

4. When the good china gets sprayed with machine-gun fire

3. That Billy Joel song mentions everybody but her husband

2. He launders millions of dollars—but try to get him to rinse out his socks

1. Certain U.S. presidents who declare war on your husband just because you wouldn't date them in high school

TOP TEN REJECTED THEMES FOR THE ICE CAPADES

10. Big Bird gets mites

9. A fat Smurf hits on Dorothy Hamill

8. Eldridge Cleaver's *Soul on Ice* on ice

7. Torvill and Dean fight over the guy who drives the Zamboni

6. Squeaky Fromme, Where Are You?

5. Snoopy Stains the Ice

4. March of the Not-Very-Masculine Ice Dancers

3. Peggy Fleming in "Ice Bitches Behind Bars"

2. Thin costumes plus cold air equals entertainment for Dad

1. True ice fishing tragedies from police files

BLITZEN'S TOP TEN
PET PEEVES

10. When airliners jettison their chemical toilets right in front of you

9. Elves who are a little too enthusiastic about putting on our harnesses

8. Dancer and Prancer always playing their Judy Garland records

7. Santa not letting us off for Jewish holidays

6. Reindeer games tainted by steroids

5. When Santa stretches out the reindeer feed with sawdust

4. The way Rudolph won't let us forget he makes twice as much as the rest of us

3. Two words: Soviet airspace

2. Swanson's Reindeer Pot Pie

1. When Santa hangs around the stable with his shirt off

TOP TEN REJECTED MODEL NAMES FOR NEW CARS

10. Pontiac Cyst

9. Dodge Glove

8. Oldsmobile Beiruter

7. Nissan Spleen

6. Chevy Junta

5. Hyundai Accordion

4. Mazda Eczema 500

3. Dodge Johnson

2. Yugo Screw Yourself

1. Ford Gelding

TOP TEN WORDS USED IN
NEW YORK POST
HEADLINES

10. Co-Ed

9. Tot

8. Horror

7. Straphangers

6. Mom

5. Weirdos

4. Hizzoner

3. Torso

2. Herr Steinbrenner

1. Slayfest/Lotto   *(tie)*

TOP TEN RECENT
SCIENTIFIC DISCOVERIES

10. Giant apes once lived in Southeast Asia

9. First crude amphibians to crawl from ocean onto dry land were looking for a towel

8. Raccoons don't really wash their food; probably lied about other things too

7. Some galaxies really only 10 feet away, but are very tiny

6. Universe expands at same rate as NBA teams

5. Fish have Country Western tunes running through their heads

4. Roy Rogers' new-style chicken is still alive when you eat it

3. Funny smell in lab was actually graduate student

2. If a blue whale gets in a fight with a giant squid, HBO has exclusive rights

1. Try topping an English muffin with bananas and honey—mmmm good!

TOP TEN REASONS DAN QUAYLE WOULD MAKE A GREAT PRESIDENT

10. Would not seem like brainy egghead when visiting our nation's injured professional wrestlers

9. Boyish good looks would cause Mrs. Gorbachev to fall in love, reveal state secrets

8. His willingness to don inspiring Eagle Man costume on national holidays

7. Secret Service agents wouldn't have to take their jobs so seriously

6. Hilarious hijinks when mischievous staffer tells him to go stand in corner of Oval Office

5. State of the Union address would be three minutes tops

4. Might really enjoy the part where after signing a bill into law, he gets to pass out a lot of souvenir pens

3. Would satisfy little-known Constitutional requirement that Chief Executive be "dumb as a tree"

2. We'd get to watch him grow up on TV

1. Impossible to pick himself for Vice President

TOP TEN BOOKSTORE PICKUP LINES

10. Care to come back to my place for a little Dickens?

9. When you're tired of dating "speed readers"—call me

8. You're pretty nicely stacked yourself

7. Have you seen a copy of *Tax Tips for Billionaires?*

6. Who's your favorite Karamazov brother?

5. I've got a great reading light next to my bed

4. I can bench-press a whole stack of James Michener novels

3. While you're turning those pages, mind if I lick your fingers?

2. You're hotter than Emily Dickinson in a tube top

1. Is that an unabridged dictionary in your pocket, or are you just glad to see me?

MRS. PAUL'S TOP TEN PET PEEVES

10. When a three-pronged tuna hook gets caught in your shoulder blade while you're casting

9. When some joker at the plant batter-dips your car keys

8. The kids aren't buying her action figure

7. Getting bread crumbs in a paper cut

6. Idiots who think she's married to the Pope

5. That bitch Betty Crocker

4. Lawsuits filed by accidentally de-boned employees

3. The flat, accusing stare of a dying cod

2. Wise guys who give you a "Here's your fish stick, lady"

1. Lackluster sales of her new cologne, "Bottom-Feeder"

TOP TEN THINGS REAGAN DOES REMEMBER

10. He used to live in a big white house

9. That bastard Sam Donaldson

8. Those great parties at Marion Barry's

7. Daughter Maureen's weight (within 150 pounds)

6. Where Nancy doesn't like to be touched

5. The name, address, and social security number of each and every one of his black supporters

4. If you need a hooker, call Bill Holden

3. 4:30—time for Wapner!

2. That Jodie Foster is a real troublemaker

1. Falling off a horse—and that's about it

TOP TEN LEAST POPULAR ARTIFICIAL INSEMINATION CLINICS

10. Stop 'n' Pop

9. Aunt Bertha's Baby Batter

8. Jimmy the Greek's Genetic Crap Shoot

7. International House of Zygotes

6. Steve Garvey's Kiddie City

5. Jack-in-the-Box

4. Cher's Bedroom

3. Ringling Brothers' Grow-Your-Own-Circus-People

2. The Port Authority

1. McFertilization

TOP TEN PERKS OF
WINNING THE
INDIANAPOLIS 500

10. Getting showered with 10W40 in locker-room celebration

9. Honorary New York City taxi license

8. Right to represent Earth in Pan-Galactic Monster Truck Rally

7. Invitation to start Mr. Gotti's car for him

6. Good chance of meeting Kamarr the Magician backstage at Letterman show

5. Don't have to shut off lights and lock up speedway like guy who finishes last

4. Get to throw one free punch at Mr. Goodwrench

3. Offers of employment from Domino's Pizza

2. Trophy, bouquet of roses, and a big wet kiss from Jim Nabors

1. All the Valvoline a guy can drink

TOP TEN MALL SHOPS
IN HELL

10. Hitler and Himmler's 31 Flavors

9. Really Painful Manicures

8. Do-the-Sharpton-Thing Hair Salon

7. Fish 'n' Lips

6. Jim Jones' Juice-a-Teria

5. Boozy, Irritable, Big and Tall Men's Shop

4. Ceaucescu's Fashion Optical

3. The Gap (Boy—they're *everywhere!*)

2. Noriega's Nut Hut (under construction)

1. Brown Julius

TOP TEN MOTHER'S DAY
GIFTS AVAILABLE IN
TIMES SQUARE

10. Rolling pin vibrator

9. "World's Greatest Mom" crack pipe

8. A lovely silk robe shoplifted from Saks

7. Videocassette of movie *Danish Moms*

6. A guy who'll do anything for fifty bucks

5. Necklace of human ears

4. Car stereo (with minor crowbar damage)

3. Combination brass knuckles/cheese slicer

2. Gift certificate good for one brutal beating

1. Inflatable Dad

TOP TEN SIGNS YOUR KID IS A LOSER

10. Neighborhood kids trade and collect his teeth

9. Sobs uncontrollably every time he sees that "Hey, Vern" guy

8. Constantly using the phrase "okie-dokie"

7. Turns you in to mall cops for parking in handicapped spot

6. Turned down for date by Cher

5. Tries to start the wave while watching game on TV

4. Pesters Eddie Albert at "Green Acres" conventions

3. When he grows up, wants to be "just like Dave"

2. Is U.S. Vice President

1. Tends to sit in the back yard and eat crickets

TOP TEN THINGS THAT WILL GET YOU THROWN OUT OF THE TRIPLE-A

10. Asking to test drive the Triple-A receptionist

9. Vomiting in a tollbooth change basket

8. Using the word *fahrvergnügen* at any time

7. Selling secret handshake to Soviets

6. Repeatedly adjusting seat belt to provide erotic stimulation

5. Calling up the office and asking, "Triple-A? How do you spell that?"

4. Lewd use of service station air hose

3. Insisting Triple-A motel guidebooks include Dave's house

2. Standing up at a meeting and shouting, "I've got a pocketful of red-hot lug nuts!"

1. Having personalized license plate reading "HOT 4 EBERT"

TOP TEN PERKS TO BEING ELECTED TO THE BASEBALL HALL OF FAME

10. Use of bullpen car for family vacations

9. Paves the way for employment in exciting field of casino greeting

8. DiMaggio himself comes over to set up your complimentary Mr. Coffee machine

7. Your restaurant may now feature Hall of Fame barbeque ribs

6. In super-secret ceremony, get to see face of guy who plays San Diego Chicken

5. "You had your chance" plaque sent to former girlfriend of your choice

4. Annual mentholated rub from Tommy Lasorda

3. Exact knowledge of how and when the world will end

2. Can go anywhere, anytime, and spit on the floor

1. When people see you on the street they say, "Hey, Hall-of-Famer!" instead of "I've already got insurance."

TOP TEN LEAST POPULAR CHRISTMAS GIFTS

10. Andre the Giant Champagne

9. Hickory Farms Smoked Gristle Assortment

8. Phil Donahue's *A Boy's First Dress*

7. An hour of free advertising on CBS

6. *The Jimmy Swaggart Pop-up Book*

5. Angry-Live-Bird-in-a-Bag from Hartz Mountain

4. Dan Rather Lather Skin Bracer for Men

3. The Living Weasel Wallet

2. Al Sharpton Hair-Styling Spackle

1. Isotoner Diapers

TOP TEN LEAST VISITED NEW YORK CITY TOURIST ATTRACTIONS

10. The Museum of Subway Odors

9. Cat Meat Cook-off

8. The Abandoned Auto Show

7. Amish peep shows

6. Chalk Body Outline Walking Tour

5. Knicks games

4. Psychotic Loner Renaissance Fair

3. Mob Informant Aqua Show

2. Mookie-Land

1. The Frozen Spit Rink

TOP TEN THINGS DAN RATHER IS AFRAID OF

10. Spiders

9. People will discover he doesn't understand maps

8. The Greenhouse Effect

7. A drunken pass by Charles Osgood's wife

6. Searing abdominal cramps during newscast

5. Endorsement deal for Bartles & Jaymes will fall through

4. Garrick Utley

3. Handshake too limp for world leaders

2. Might giggle during Chernobyl update

1. "West 57th" kids laugh behind his back

TOP TEN OFF-SEASON
SPORTS ON ESPN

10. Uninflated basketball

9. Fat-guy hackysack

8. No-hands auto racing

7. Shirts-and-skins speed typing

6. Amish rake fights

5. Miniature horseshoes

4. Dropping cows from planes

3. Padded suit lumber swat

2. Oprah tipping

1. Dog hockey

TOP TEN QUESTIONS
PEOPLE ASK PAUL SHAFFER

10. What's Dave really like?

9. What's Anton Fig really like?

8. Can you get me tickets to "Donahue"?

7. So what have you been doing since "Saturday Night Live"?

6. Are those "Stump the Band" people for real?

5. Honey, are you ashamed of me and the kids?

4. Would you like fries with that?

3. Are you sure this is your credit card, Mr. Walsh?

2. So why did you pick Letterman to co-host your show?

1. When the bride and groom enter, could you play "We've Only Just Begun"?

TOP TEN REALLY NICE THINGS ABOUT NEW YORK IN THE SUMMER

10. Abundant wonderland of unidentifiable smells

9. Out-of-towners overjoyed by secret hope that maybe they'll get to manage Yankees

8. Air-conditioned comfort of bright, shiny, well-appointed subway cars

7. Mayor usually out of town on "business"

6. Warm thin air enables stray bullets to travel farther

5. First-run Broadway plays waive "no shirt, no shoes, no service" policy

4. Giant heat-seeking batlike lizards swarm skyscrapers at night

3. Most cab drivers, in lieu of tip, gladly accept gentle kiss on forehead

2. Bobbing corpses in East River make perfect water-ski slalom course

1. Tattoos, tattoos, tattoos

TOP TEN LEAST POPULAR ROADSIDE ATTRACTIONS

10. Geraldo-Land

9. Arena Football Hall of Fame

8. Stump Johnson's World of Angry Animals

7. World's Largest Spit Sink

6. Catch-Your-Own-Wasp Ranch

5. Recreation of Vin Scully's boyhood home

4. One-Eyed Elf Dodgeball Cage

3. You-Hit-It, We-Cook-It Roadkill Grill

2. The Enchanted Mitten

1. Giant Shirtless Santa Claus

TOP TEN REVELATIONS IN ALBERT GOLDMAN'S UPCOMING BIOGRAPHY OF RINGO

10. Only Beatle to portray himself in *Beatlemania*

9. Used to give John and Paul token songs to sing so they wouldn't feel left out

8. Had a secretary named Lincoln, while Lincoln had a secretary named Ringo

7. For a while, actually believed Paul was dead

6. Served in Indiana National Guard during Vietnam War

5. Suggested "Hey, Hey, We're the Monkees" as Beatles theme song

4. On their honeymoon, he and Barbara Bach held a "bed-in" to promote Seagram's wine coolers

3. Made a fortune selling cheesy Ginsu Knife sets on TV (I'm sorry—that's revelations about *Ronco*)

2. Advised Paul that "Hey, Dude" just didn't sound right

1. Vocal on "Octopus's Garden" played backwards sounds like "Thank God these other guys are so talented"

TOP TEN LIES WE TELL OUR GUESTS

10. Don't worry, there are still lots of people watching at 1:25 A.M.

9. Those *are* clean towels

8. Sure, Dave would love to sing a duet with you

7. We invited you here because we've wanted to have you on for a long, long time and not at all because our other guests canceled and we're really desperate, Regis

6. Relax, he's not the same guy who does Dave's hair

5. We brought you here on a bus so you'd have more funny stories to tell

4. Dave saw your movie—and loved it!

3. Dave saw your movie

2. We'll edit that out later

1. They're not booing, they're chanting "Dave"

TOP TEN REJECTED
JEOPARDY CATEGORIES

10. Things That Ooze

9. Deathbed Pranks

8. Noises Dad Makes

7. What's That? Ham?

6. Things You Just Want to Pound and Pound with a Shovel

5. Doorknob Lore

4. Leading Men Who Are Really Gay

3. Presidential Salads

2. Items Found in Wadded-up Napkins

1. Moist Things

Roman Numeral Two!

TOP TEN LISTS
from "LATE NIGHT with
DAVID LETTERMAN"

**LIKE WATCHING TV IN
CONVENIENT BOOK FORM!**

Also available now in
paperback from
Pocket Books

POCKET
B O O K S

1027